Christians lived with growing hostility and misunderstanding at the time of Peter's writing. He called them "God's elect, strangers in the world." But even though Christ had left them behind, God did not leave them alone; He gave them everything they needed for time and eternity—He gave them the same Power that raised Christ from the grave, just because they were believers in His only Son. Peter is talking to us in a world that can still be a tough place to live in. We have that same Power with us today that guarantees a joy-filled life through our faith, our hope and love as related to Christ.

But all this power from God calls forth some requirements on our part. Among them is that we be holy, because God is holy, and that we build on certain values which God has given us. By following these two requirements we will attain a spiritual growth that evidences life and health in the Spirit.

In our lives on earth, Peter calls for us to build on the rock-hard foundation of Christ; to lean heavily upon the support of our brothers in Christ; to live as servants and disciples of the living Christ. Peter tells the people of his day how to function in a secular society that was pagan, unjust, and ready to afflict misery on the Christian community. Times really haven't changed much. Even in "Christian" America we are faced with these same enemies. But Peter tells how Christians can live for God's glory, even when the going gets tough!

When the Going Gets Tough

D. Stuart Briscoe

Regal
Books
A Division of GL Publications
Ventura, CA U.S.A.

The foreign language publishing of all Regal books is under the direction of GLINT. GLINT provides financial and technical help for the adaptation, translation and publishing of books for millions of people worldwide. For information regarding translation, contact: GLINT, P.O. Box 6688, Ventura, California 93006.

Published by Regal Books
A Division of GL Publications
Ventura, California 93006
Printed in U.S.A.

Library of Congress Cataloging in Publication Data
Briscoe, D. Stuart.
    When the going gets tough.
        1. Bible. N.T. Peter, 1st—Criticism, interpretation, etc.
2. Christian life—
1960-   I. Title.
BS2795.2.B74 1982 227'.92077   82-11205
ISBN 0-8307-0802-2

CONTENTS

ONE

WHEN THE GOING GETS TOUGH
1 Peter 1:1-2

Bearded, bedraggled men bearing signs stating, "The end is near" have long been the subject of cartoonists. People have laughed and gone on their way; but recently the mood has changed. Many of the laughers, while they may not anticipate "the end," are certainly not too happy about the present, mainly because life has become increasingly difficult. With the breakdown of marriage, the pressures of inflationary spirals, the increase in violence and the threat of nuclear destruction, more and more people are finding that the going is getting tough.

Numerous solutions have been sought and suggested ranging from blatantly political to the downright farcical. Some see "supply side economics" as the answer; others advocate "Get right with God"; "Get a gun and lay aside 12-months' dry food." Those with a tendency to despair have found much fuel for their flames while those who prefer a positive approach have followed such prophets of hope as Howard Ruff explaining "how to prosper in the coming hard times."

Contrary to the teaching of some misguided enthusiasts, Christians have not been exempt from hard times and are required to handle the rough issues of life in a unique fashion, alongside those who make no Christian profession. They will not do this, however, if they model their responses on secular patterns and derive their encouragement from non-biblical sources.

Peter wrote his "First Epistle" in a rough situation which he rightly suspected would get tougher. His intent in writing to the small churches scattered throughout the inhospitable regions of Asia Minor was to warn the believers of their impending difficulties, to encourage them in their spiritual position and to practically encourage them to live Christianly in invidious circumstances.

Sulpicius Severus, the Roman historian, tells us that Peter was crucified during the reign of Nero, after the fire which destroyed half the city. The emperor, whose unpopularity had been well earned, was widely suspected of arson but managed to divert suspicion to the Christians who were themselves easy prey for his malicious slander. They were horribly persecuted even to the extent that "new kinds of death were invented" as they were "devoured by dogs" and some were "set apart . . . that when the day came to a close, they should be consumed to serve for light." Eventually, it was decreed by Rome that it was "unlawful to be a Christian." How much of this persecution was foreseen by Peter before he was himself consumed by it we have no way of knowing; but it would appear that he was well aware that the going was tough in Rome and would probably become equally tough for the believers scattered throughout the provinces. With this in mind he wrote: "Peter, an apostle of Jesus Christ, to God's elect, strangers in the world, scattered throughout Pontus, Galatia, Cappadocia, Asia and Bithynia, who have been chosen according to the foreknowledge of God the Father, through the sanctifying work of the Spirit, for obedience to Jesus Christ and sprinkling by his blood: Grace and peace be yours in abundance" (1 Pet. 1:1,2).

The positive tone of the letter is evident in the opening words of customary introduction. Identifying himself as "Peter, an apostle of Jesus Christ," the writer promptly reminded his readers of the dramatic demonstration of God's power in his life. Carefully using the name given to him by the Master, which predicted that he would become a rock despite all his natural tendencies to the contrary, the writer directed the attention of his readers to the fact that what he had to say was credible because it was a man changed by the power of God who was speaking.

We use the expression "Jesus Christ" almost as if Jesus was His Christian name and Christ His family name, but we must remember that Jesus was the name which means "saviour," and "Christ" was the title which only God's chosen and anointed Messiah could rightly use. False messiahs have come and gone but, for Peter, Jesus of Nazareth was the One whom God had sent as His anointed Redeemer. Once again in the opening words of the letter the presence of the power of God in the affairs of men is emphasized.

To claim the title of "apostle" was to claim a special relationship with Christ. The word *apostle* is simply an anglicization of the Greek word *apostolos* which means "a person sent with full authority." Peter was not at all bashful in this claim and it is apparent that the primitive church had no difficulty in accepting that he did indeed speak with authority in the name of Christ. The writer of the letter is worth listening to because (1) the changed life points to his credibility, (2) his conviction concerning Jesus being Christ exudes authenticity and (3) his apostolic office brings a touch of authority to all he had to say. People living in rough times need such a messenger.

The recipients of the letter lived in a far-flung region of the Roman Empire covering the area now belonging to Turkey. How the churches in these regions were established we do not know for certain except that Paul and his companions certainly traveled in the area preaching and teaching. Also people from these provinces were among the crowds on the Day of Pentecost who heard Peter preach and, presumably, some of them believed and returned home with the message of Christ.

There is no doubt that life was not easy in those days, particularly for Christians living under Roman domination; but Peter spoke of his readers in glowing terms designed to take their minds off their troubles and place them firmly on their privileges. "God's elect, strangers in the world," he called them. In Old Testament times Jehovah chose a people for Himself through whom He would make known Himself and His purposes for mankind. He called them "my people, my chosen [ones], the people I formed for myself" (Isa. 43:20,21). Peter applied similar terms to the believers in his day with the intention of reminding them that, as the children of Israel were called to be God's elite corps, so they, in the midst of their problems, were similarly "God's elect"; and it was through them that God intended to continue His redemptive work.

Years ago when I was a member of the Royal Marines I marveled at the way tired and dispirited troops could be raised to new heights of endeavor and involvement by the simple expedient of reminding us of the elite corps to which we belonged, the remarkable heritage of which we were a part, and the expectations which rested upon us because we wore the same uniform as those who had gone before.

Peter went on to describe his readers as "strangers in the world," no doubt emphasizing something with which they were at times painfully familiar, namely that their Christian profession, of necessity, put them at odds with the surrounding society.

The popular games at Rome had become so violent and cruel that Christians had felt compelled to disassociate themselves from such forms of entertainment. They had also declined to engage in the worship activities which involved the plethora of Roman gods. The Christian stance in these matters was deeply resented. Being against the national sport then, as now, was not conducive to popularity. Taking a stand against the national religion was no more popular; and the fact that the religion was also bound up in concepts of nationalism meant that those who were against the national religion were often regarded as being, in some way, against the state. Pity the people in any society who take unpopular stands on the three most volatile issues—sports, politics and religion!

At first the Christians were regarded as oddities who would eventually go away. But as time went on and they refused to go away, benign neglect turned to virulent opposition and the believers, at best, were ostracized and, at worst, liquidated. When Peter called them the "scattered" people he was using a word which contained several nuances of meaning. It referred to the unfortunate circumstances of sheep being scattered or of chaff being blown by the winds, and no doubt the scattered believers of the early church often felt like lost sheep and windblown chaff. But seed was also scattered with very positive, fruitful results; and there was no doubt that Christians soon learned that the unpleasantness of being scattered could lead to most fruitful results if they looked at their situation as being a strategic planting by the hand of God. Again the idea of privilege in the affairs of the Most High comes through most clearly.

Human beings have an understandable tendency to look at things from a human perspective. While it is an understandable tendency, it must be seen as a distorted perspective. Peter, who had done more than his share of looking at things from his own vantage point, and on one particularly painful occasion had been roundly rebuked for it, had learned the hard way to see things from the divine angle. This comes through powerfully as he reminds his readers of the work of God in their lives. It is particularly noteworthy that he specifically outlined the work of each member of the Trinity—Father, Son and Holy Spirit.

One of the most important distinctions that must be made is in people's understanding of salvation. Because great emphasis is often placed on the necessity for human decision, it is not uncommon for people to view their salvation as something basically dependent on their decision. The problem with this emphasis is that humans know how frail and fickle humans are, and if they look at their salvation as something related to their capability they may wander and waver in their relationship to the Lord. However, the balancing truth clearly emphasized in Scripture insists that our salvation is dependent on the initiative and decision of God, both of which precede any action of man. Peter emphasized this with the words "chosen according to the foreknowledge of God the Father." God's foreknowledge or *prognosis*—for that is the Greek word—is the basis of His choice. Anyone who has had dealings with a physician knows something about diagnosis and prognosis. Once we have been made aware of the problem we usually want to know what the doctor believes will happen. He will probably give his opinion (or prognosis) which will be an educated guess based on experience and statistics; but he of all people knows how wrong he may be.

The prognosis of God is not a guess and does not depend on statistical analysis of what has previously happened. His foreknowledge is based on what He has determined to do, and nothing will stop either Him or His plan. He freely determined to offer salvation to the ungodly; freely determined to make it available through His Son; determined that through faith in Him and His work on the Cross redemption would be available; and freely decided that those who put their faith in Christ would have eternal life and would reign with Him forever. Not one ounce of pressure was brought to bear on the Father in any of these decisions. They were all His, and He is totally committed to making sure that things work out the way He decided. These decisions, you will note, do not discount human accountability or cancel human choice. For God has chosen to require human cooperation in His salvation plan as surely as He decided in the first place to make salvation available. The great benefit of this aspect of truth to those for whom the going is tough is that they realize that in the final analysis their salvation is not dependent solely on them but rather is based solidly on the immutable purposes of the Sovereign Lord. Therein lies great security for troubled believers.

The Holy Spirit, as Peter pointed out, also plays a massive role in our salvation particularly in His "sanctifying work." Sanctify is a word used very little today but it is related to "holy" and "saint" in New Testament usage and has the meaning "to set apart." Buildings, people, vessels, animals were all said to be sanctified which means that they had a specific function for which they were suited and to which they were committed. Believers are to understand that when the Holy Spirit enters their lives at regeneration they are immediately "set apart" in that they now possess His special presence and are specially possessed by Him for His purposes. This we can call initial sanctification, but we must not forget the continual sanctification which Scripture teaches. Once set apart for Him the believer needs to recognize the necessity of behaving differently; in fact, behaving in a manner which is compatible with the new standing. This new behavior is the result of continual "sanctifying work" of the Spirit. The end of this ongoing experience comes when finally, in the risen Lord's presence we see Him and become like Him. But until then the sanctifying work goes on.

When Lady Diana Spencer became engaged to the Prince of Wales she was immediately "set apart" as the one who would become the next queen. It soon became clear, however, that she was not used to the peculiar pressures that such an exalted position entailed; but as time went on, through careful tutoring and nurturing by people skilled in such matters, she began to exhibit the poise and command expected of someone in her position. No doubt there were times when she wondered if she would ever make it, but like the "set apart" Christian she had to realize that her position was not dependent on her performance, but because her position was secure, she was powerfully motivated to perform appropriately.

The work of the Son is presented as "sprinkling by his blood." The Old Testament imagery contained in this expression is related to the Old Testament sacrificial system where the life of the victim was forfeited that sin might be forgiven and judgment averted. It is significant that the blood of the sacrifice was collected and applied to the doorposts in the case of the Passover, or to the extremities of the high priest's body, because this demonstrated that formal observation of a sacrificial act was not enough. There had to be a personal application of the merits of the sacrifice.

So it is with the believer—he must know that there has been an intimate experience of forgiveness and a deeply personal knowledge of reconciliation on the basis of Christ's sacrifice. This knowledge fits the believer for a life of special relationship to the Lord which is based on loving obedience. The statement that we are "chosen . . . for obedience" should not be overlooked, particularly when the going gets tough.

Doubtless there were many times when the Christians to whom the pressures of Rome were all too real would have found disobedience much less physically painful than obedience, and submission to Rome much more amenable than obedience to Christ. But knowing they were called to obedience right from the outset of their spiritual experience they recognized that their commitment to obedience was all part of their sprinkling through His blood. In the frightening days in which they lived they not only needed the soul anchor which only their knowledgeable experience of Christ could give them, but they also looked for a practical endowment of the "grace and peace" which the formal traditional introduction to the letter wished them. Peace in the midst of political and societal turmoil; grace to handle the overwhelming pressures to which they would be subjected in the near future, if Peter's prediction of the "fiery trial" (1 Pet. 4:12, *KJV*) proved correct.

There is much material and many counselors available to those who are experiencing rough times; but in the long run only the truth of God found in Scripture can equip people for the difficult times, because only the eternal Word provides the context in which temporal problems can be understood, and only the eternal Lord can supply the resources which human problems demand.

TWO

A POSITIVE ATTITUDE
1 Peter 1:3-5

I've never heard of a seminar on the developing of bad attitudes, but I've seen a lot of seminars being made available on how to develop good attitudes. Now I wonder why that is? Perhaps it's because we have a natural tendency towards bad attitudes, aided by the circumstances in which we live, the environment in which we have been raised, and the situations that we are required to confront; therefore, it is necessary for us to develop good attitudes because they don't just happen. But before we can even begin to develop them there must be the desire for a good attitude, because in some situations we develop attitudes which are so bad that we have no desire to change.

Do you remember the story of the man who was lying by the pool of Bethesda? He had been disabled for 38 years. The Lord Jesus went up to him and asked him, "Do you want to get well?" (John 5:6). The question appears strange because we would assume that his sole objective in lying by the pool was to be healed. It is possible, however, that the Lord Jesus asked the question because He knew that the man had an attitudinal problem. He had probably come to the point of despair, and the Lord recognized that there was nothing He could do for him if the man really didn't desire to be made whole.

Quite often we give up because of difficult circumstances, because of the complexity of the situation, because of the apparent absence of solutions. We stop trying to rectify anything and just allow all our circumstances to overwhelm us, our situations to take control of us, and our natural tendencies to pull us down. But somewhere along the line we need to get around to desiring to be different. How does that come about?

Developing a Positive Attitude

Believers begin to develop positive attitudes because, *first*, they have a solid grasp of divine truth—*the revealed Word of God to their hearts*. For example, notice how the Apostle Peter, referring to God's work in our lives, says, "In his great mercy he has given us new birth into a living hope through the resurrection of Jesus Christ from the dead" (1 Pet. 1:3). This thought of a "living hope" springs to Peter's mind as soon as he starts writing.

The Scriptures teach that by nature we are dead to God. The only thing that is of any help to dead people is new life. God, recognizing our spiritual deadness, made it possible for Christ to die and rise again for us. He promised that this risen Lord Jesus would be made available to us in the person of the Holy Spirit and that He would come into our lives and spark newness of life within us, and it would be just like being "born again"—born from above. This is probably the earliest occasion the expression "born again" is used in Scripture; the well-known reference in John 3 would be written at least 30 years after Peter's Epistle.

It is unfortunate that a lot of people spend a lot of time arguing about the born-again experience. They want to know the when and the how without realizing that the reality of being born again is shown not by careful rehearsing of the details surrounding the experience but by clear evidence of new life. People don't come to me and question whether I'm alive on the basis of my recollections of my original birthday. They appear to accept the fact of my birth because of the reality of my life. The important thing about being born again is that we are living anew in the same way the important thing about being born is that we are alive! God has moved into our lives in remarkable fashion and He has infused us with newness of life, making us a new creation, and we will never be the same again. It is a gift we didn't deserve, we can never earn, and can never pay off. It is something that God freely decided to give to human beings who were lost in sin, at emnity with God. Out of His great mercy He gave us newness of life.

They tell us that "hope springs eternal in the human breast!" I don't know about the "eternal" but I do know that people demonstrate a determined need for something to hope for. Every four years we elect a new president, pinning all our hopes upon him, only to be disappointed repeatedly but determined to try again!

The believers have a hope that is not going to be raised to be dashed—*it is, second, a hope that is overwhelmingly confident.* It is something that

God has built into our lives, rooted in the fact that having been given Christ we can be sure God will give us all things that we need related to Christ. "He who did not spare his own Son, but gave him up for us all—how will he not also, along with him, graciously give us all things?" (Rom. 8:32). Paul's question is rhetorical—no answer is necessary because the answer is obvious. If He gave us Christ to live within us, and we're born again through His indwelling presence, what can we possibly imagine God would be thinking about if He didn't give us everything we need—along with Christ—for time and eternity!? When we understand this, there is hope. But it's not hope in humanity; it's hope in deity.

Peter goes a step further, as he reminds us that "he has given us new birth into a living hope through the resurrection of Jesus Christ from the dead" (1 Pet. 1:3). Why do we pin our hopes on God doing something certain and sure for us? The answer is, because of "the resurrection." There is an air of solid certainty about the believer's hope. I like to look at it this way. I have problems; I look at them, try to understand them, evaluate them and then quickly remind myself that God had a problem. His problem was that His Son, whom He ordained should be King of kings and Lord of lords, was unfortunately dead. God however addressed the problem in superlative fashion—He raised Him from the dead. Now then, whenever we confront problems we relate them to God's simple and dramatic solution of His problems and say, "God, you are the God of my problems as well as my successes. You are the God of my beginning and my end and everything in between, which means that I can relate this problem to you. Knowing what you do with problems I am confident you can certainly handle this one." The believer's hope is born of confidence based on the historical fact that God raised up Christ from the dead!

Peter's positive approach to life is also related to, third, his understanding of the gift of a new status. He says not only have we been born again into a living hope but we've also been born again into "an inheritance," and that means that we have become "heirs of God and co-heirs with Christ" (Rom. 8:17).

It is highly probable that the words Peter heard from the Master's lips by Galilee were echoing in his heart—"Do not store up for yourselves treasures on earth, where moth and rust destroy, and where thieves break in and steal. But store up for yourselves treasures in heaven, where moth and rust do not destroy, and where thieves do not break in and steal" (Matt. 6:19,20). Then He added these pungent words—"For where your treasure is, there your heart will be also" (v. 21). Perhaps Peter is thinking of the change in his own perspective from a life absorbed with fishing nets, a leaky old boat and some stinky fish and the salt to pack them in, to a life of bigger and grander and greater things. God had given him the insight into what it means to be a son of God, an heir of God, an eternal creature. He had given him a vista of heaven, and a sense of spiritual values.

I have a particular delight in sermons which have three points, preferably alliterative! In Peter I find a kindred spirit, for he described the inheritance as follows: *aphthartos*—incorruptible, *amiantos*—undefiled, *amarantos*—unfading (see 1 Pet. 1:4). He is simply taking what Jesus said in the Sermon on the Mount about moth, rust and thieves and showing the security and certainty of the inheritance because it is "kept in heaven." The strength of the word *kept* is apparent when we remember that *keep* can also mean that part of a castle into which people under attack could run for survival. In the keep they were literally "kept"!

It's amazing what a good attitude believers can have when we understand our status and the unassailable security of the inheritance to which we are entitled! *Added to this is, fourth, the gift of a new security* which Peter describes as follows: "Who through faith are shielded by God's power until the coming of the salvation that is ready to be revealed in the last time" (v. 5). There are three tenses of salvation. It is possible for a person to say, "I have been saved," but it is equally necessary for a person to say, "I am being saved" and in addition to predict, "I will be saved." These statements appear to be contradictory unless we realize we are saved from different things. When we say "I have been saved" we mean we have been saved from sin's penalty—we have been forgiven—our sin has been reckoned to Christ, Christ's righteousness has been reckoned to us, and we can look the world in the eye and say, "Folks, take a good, long, hard look. There is a saved sinner standing in front of you."

Believers have a problem with the power of their sinful nature, but God graciously makes it possible for us to overcome that old power of sin within us so that we can, on a daily basis, say, "I am being saved progressively." There are things in my life that are not there to the same extent that they were 12 months ago. That's growth, that's maturity, that's development, that's progress which can be explained by the fact that we are being saved through the power of the Spirit from those things. In a healthy spiritual experience we should be sensing that from the moment we have been saved, we are being saved.

Peter adds that we are, through faith, shielded by God's power unto the coming of the salvation that is ready to be revealed in the last time. He is talking about ultimately being saved from sin's presence. In "the last time" the Lord Jesus will come and take His people to be with Him, and the heavens and earth will dissolve with fervent heat, as Peter states in his second Epistle. Then we'll say, "Praise God you have saved me from sin's penalty, you did go on saving me from sin's power, and now the whole thing is finished. You have saved me from sin's presence and I live in a realm wherein dwell righteousness and justice."

Now think of these things for a minute. If God has already said we have been saved in order that, progressively, we might grow more and more like the Lord Jesus as we are being saved, and He knows that this progression will find its completion when Christ comes again and we are saved from sin's presence, isn't it reasonable to assume that if God started it He will finish it? If salvation means anything, it means salvation in its entirety from the penalty and the power and the presence of sin; so if He started it we can be confident that He will continue it and complete it. Therein lies our security.

Now notice we are "shielded by God's power" (v. 5). Having already linked our "hope" to the historical fact of the Resurrection, Peter links our security to the power of God which was demonstrated in such undeniable and exhilarating fashion in the same event. Believers, fearful of their situation when under pressure, need look only to the Resurrection for assurance that God's power is adequate in their case. However, the power is operative in our lives "through faith," which means "you have got to believe it to enjoy it."

It may be a surprise to realize that the way to produce good attitudes in people is to teach them good theology. Teaching, of course, requires learning, and this comes only as we make sure that we constantly study the truth. If we don't, we will come under the gravitational pull of everything around us and in no time we will be down again with those who do not know the truth.

It is also vital that we should have constant reminders of the truth and continual encouragement to apply the truth that we know. When this is clear we will have no problem seeing that the church of Jesus Christ must be a community where there is a solid diet of the teaching of the Word of God; a community in which interpersonal relationships are developed so that we can encourage each other; and a community in which we have such loving communication with people that they can remind us when we're "off the wall," correct us, turn us around and help us to build the positive attitudes which are so necessary. Our society today is riddled with bad attitudes on every hand—suspicion, distrust, people being ripped off, abuse, selfishness, egocentricity, latent violence—they are all there. In the church of Jesus Christ we need to get our theology squared away and encourage each other to apply it so that we begin to have some good, solid, healthy attitudes, in stark contrast to the world around us.

Demonstrating a Positive Attitude

Peter suspects he may not have long until his head is separated from the rest of him, or he is crucified upside down; but you would never guess it from his buoyant words: "Praise be to the God and Father of our Lord Jeus Christ!" (v. 3). A positive attitude is often demonstrated by praise and, in Peter's case, his objective in recounting the truths with which his readers are familiar is to get them to join him. They should praise because in His great mercy God gave him new birth, a living hope and an inheritance. They can praise Him that it won't perish, it will never spoil, it will never corrupt, and it is reserved in heaven for them. They can also praise Him because He has given them His own power to shield them and He will complete the salvation He started. When their enemies have done their worst, which could possibly mean death, it will mean an early introduction to their eternal inheritance.

Unfortunately there is a tendency for believers to not relate to their theology when things get tough but to become absorbed with the rough situation and the search for a quick solution. At this time we must center on who God is, what He has done, what He is doing, and particularly on what He is going to do. Praise has to be intelligently rooted in truth rather than floated on fantasy. Nothing worries me more than to have some unthinking, insensitive person come and slap a troubled believer on the back and say, "Praise the Lord"! When people are going through deep waters we need to get in the deep water with them, not voice silly, inane expressions that demonstrate our own superficiality, but to remind them of their theology when they are ready to be encouraged.

You'll also notice that Peter, despite his difficulties, uses the word *hope*. Believers, in addition to being praising people when the going gets rough, should be filled with an expectant hope. Peter also shows that Christians should have an exuberant faith because we're kept by the power of God through faith. Praise, hope and faith are the stuff of which the positive attitude is made and the means whereby it is exhibited.

I long to see the church of Jesus Christ getting way out ahead of our society and producing people with a positive attitude because, quite frankly, anybody can be negative, anybody can be destructive, anybody can be divisive. One evening after there had been a lot of criticism of one aspect of the ministry at the board meeting the chairman, Virgil Staples, said very quietly, "It's a well-established fact that any jackass can kick down a barn but it takes a craftsman to build one." Then he added, "Are there any craftsmen?" There are plenty of jackasses who are kicking everything to pieces, and they find their targets in many churches. My question is this, "Are there any craftsmen?" Thank God there are. You can tell them by their attitudes.

THREE

JOY-FILLED LIVING
1 Peter 1:6-9

The American Declaration of Independence states that human beings have the inalienable right to life, liberty, and the pursuit of happiness, and there is little doubt that considerable time and energy have been spent both at government and individual levels to ensure the happiness of the people. That the effort has not met with conspicuous success is one of the great puzzles confronting the nation's leadership. Part of the problem is that human happiness too often depends on happenings. If the happenings don't happen to happen we are unhappy. There is, therefore, a great emphasis on the control of environment, the solving of problems and the manipulation of circumstances with a view to making sure that all the happenings happen to happen the way we happen to want them to happen on the understanding that we will then be happy. Actually it's a fantasy wrapped in futility! If it was possible to organize happenings so they happen to happen the way we happen to want them to happen, boredom—not happiness—would be the result.

The Bible themes of joy in suffering and peace in conflict are much more realistic both in light of the failure of our organized society to produce happy people and the impossibility of the search for ways to produce the ideal state wherein happiness reigns supreme. Peter's first Epistle is a marvelous illustration of the Christian experience of joy, written, as it was, against the somber background of persecution and suffering. He is writing to warn his readers of the fiery trial that will come upon them, but he also outlines his expectation that they will experience a quality of joy that can be described only as inexpressible and glorious. Far from being the product of circumstances which could produce only pain and anguish, this joy will transcend their circumstances because it is related to something infinitely more stable and secure.

Peter informs his readers that their joy will come through their faith, their hope and their love. This familiar trilogy—faith, hope and love—which many people think was Paul's specialty, in actual fact is that which Peter speaks of too. Inexpressible and glorious joy, then, is related to faith and love, and most emphatically not circumstances. That is one of the most powerful lessons Christians need to learn and be reminded of, and it is one of the most powerful Christian distinctives that needs to be modeled before a happiness-crazed society.

The Joy That Comes Through Faith

It is *the ground of faith* which determines the results of faith. Great faith in an unworthy object produces despair and disaster. You can commit yourself wholeheartedly to thin ice and drown by faith. On the other hand, little faith in very thick ice can be as safe as standing on reinforced concrete.

You notice that Peter says, "In this you greatly rejoice" (v. 6). In what? The answer is found in the preceding five verses. First, he speaks of the revelation of the Father's mercy. God has freely chosen to treat sinful humanity with mercy. It is a divine initiative, it is a divine truth, it is a divine revelation, and when we know it and believe it we rejoice.

Second, he points out the result of the Son's ministry. He has sprinkled us with His blood. The benefits of His death have been applied to our lives, resulting in the forgiveness of sins and reconciliation to God.

Third, there is the promise of the Son's return in great glory to incorporate His people in His eternal kingdom. When we see Him we will be like Him, and our eternal destiny is secure. In this we rejoice!

Fourth, he talks about the sanctifying work of the Holy Spirit. There is clear evidence of His impact upon the believers in the changing, converting work that He has accomplished. The ground of faith is the God who is totally committed to being God, has acted on our behalf, offered us what we don't deserve—we have taken it and been changed by it, and therefore our faith is in who God is and what He is doing. This means there is one constant factor in a world that is full of uncertainties and inconsistencies. What is that factor? That God is totally committed to being *God*. Those who know this rejoice through faith.

Peter goes on to talk about *the growth of faith*. He says, "You greatly rejoice, though now for a little while you may have had to suffer grief in all kinds of trials" (v. 6). Presumably the "little while" and the "grief" and "all kinds of trials" refer to the time of Nero's persecution. This grief is not the product of callous, cold fate but is related to the God of whom he has spoken so warmly. He sees the trials as being purposeful in the context of God's work in his life and theirs. The purpose is explained as follows: "These have come so that your faith . . . may be proved genuine and may result in praise, glory and honor when Jesus Christ is revealed" (v. 7). As faith is firmly grounded, joy is established—as faith grows, joy flourishes; so the merciful God allows His children to go through times that are tough so that their faith can grow.

Faith is more precious than gold. The commodity everybody thinks is the most valuable, in actual fact is not. In Peter's folio gold is far inferior to faith grounded in who God is and what God is doing. He adds the thought that their faith is going to be tested so that they can really find out how valuable it is. How do we find out if faith is more valuable than gold? We may be confronted with the choice between making a fast buck at the expense of a principle related to Christian faith, or standing for the principle at the expense of the buck. This, to Peter, would not seem to be a "fiery trial," but our faith might be singed by it!

What about health? Is it possible that health can be more important than faith? How will we know? One of these days we may get sick, and our reaction will show very quickly what's more important, faith or health. The fiery trial of bad health has destroyed the faith of some and refined the faith of others, and in so doing has shown the real nature of faith. We find out the value of our faith by putting it to the test, and Peter insists that God is about to help them in the evaluation process.

Not only is our faith more important than gold but *the testing of our faith* is more important than the refining of gold. There is a commodity called "fool's gold" which isn't gold at all. It looks like it, but it is actually an iron commodity. It is neces- sary to "fire" gold to find out if it is real gold or fool's gold. In the same way that there is a refining of gold, there must be a refining of faith.

I wonder if Peter's mind, as he is writing, is going back to the days when the Lord Jesus said to him, "Simon, Satan has asked for you. He wants to sift you like wheat" (see Luke 22:31). Even a fisherman like Simon knew how farmers on the hillside behind the lake handled the harvest. They threw the grain up in the air so that the chaff was blown away in the wind. Satan had asked for the chance to get at the disciples and hurl them up in the air to disorient them, throw them around, kick them about, and the Master had given per- mission but added, "I'm praying that your faith won't fail." It was probably common knowledge to the Christians in Asia Minor that Peter, on that awful night of the crucifixion, had denied Christ three times. But he had emerged from the fiery trial, held by the prayers of the Lord, a sadder and wiser man—sad about his lack of faith, wise about the limits of his faith. He had found out that most of his faith was in himself, and that spelled disas- ter. He had said, "Even though all of them forsake you, I won't," only to discover that his noble inten- tions would not be matched by noble achievement—a sad but glorious discovery which only the fiery trial could reveal. That night the air was full of Peter's chaff but not long after the real faith began to show.

Then we must consider *the goal of faith*: "These have come so that your faith . . . may be proved genuine and may result in praise, glory and honor when Jesus Christ is revealed" (1 Pet. 1:7). He calls the goal of faith "the salvation of . . . souls" (v. 9) which we are receiving, but which we also look forward to receiving. This paradoxical concept is similar—and related—to the truth that Christ has come but is yet to come. We have now in Christ our salvation, but only when we see Christ in glory will we receive all we have in Him.

While everything is easy, everything is fun, everything is fine, people naturally concentrate on the pleasant here and now. But when the easy becomes hard, and the fun becomes tears, and the fine becomes rough, thought patterns change dramatically. Questions like, Where am I heading? What's going to happen? To whom do I belong? abound. If there is a spiritual orientation the answers will come from the biblical truths concerning the return in glory of the risen Lord and the exciting prospects of sharing in the glory. But it is a sad truth that it sometimes requires the testing of our faith to bring us to the point of interest in the goal of our faith.

For some of us life is just beautiful, sweet, sunshine and butterflies. Fiery trials, Jesus coming again, heaven, the trial of faith are subjects of little interest. But those of you whose lives are full of the pleasantries where the butterflies flutter by must know that the fiery trial will come. The going will get tough, so learn these things now so that having learned them, when you need them the Holy Spirit will bring them to remembrance.

The Joy That Comes Through Hope

There is a great note of hope in what Peter is saying here.

First, notice the *hope that comes through comparison*. For example in verse 6 Peter says, "Though now for *a little while* you may have had to suffer grief . . ." (italics added). When we're in the midst of suffering or trial or temptation or difficulty, "interminable" sounds more relevant than "a little while." Is there no end to this? Is there no light at the end of the tunnel? Is there no way of easing the pain? Will I ever get over this trauma? Can I ever forgive and forget what has happened to me? The interminable present becomes "a little while" for Peter when seen in relation to "the last time" which will introduce the whole of eternity. Eyes fixed on the little while here see only interminable and overwhelming difficulties. On the other hand, the unpleasant now, seen in the light of the last times, is touched with rays of hope as transforming as the touch of dawn on the darkness of the night. Joy is to be found in this kind of hope.

Peter speaks of the "grief" they will suffer in the same context as the "sprinkled blood" of the Lord Jesus. Some of them, including Peter and Paul, will have their blood shed as martyrs; but there will be an involuntary aspect to their deaths in marked contrast to Christ laying down His life for them. Peter can compare the little while of suffering now to the last days of all that lies ahead of him, and he can also compare the sufferings that they are going through with the sufferings that Christ endured. Jeremiah, the weeping prophet, spoke prophetically of our Lord, "Look around and see. Is any suffering like my suffering?" (Lam. 1:12). And the answer is no. There is no sorrow like His, no agony like His, no passion like His. And how did His agony and His sorrow and His passion end? In a glorious resurrection! What is the end of our suffering and grief for a little while? A glorious resurrection. Therein lies hope, the seedpod of joy.

Peter goes on to compare "gold, which perishes" with an inheritance that "can never perish, spoil or fade—[reserved and] kept in heaven" for us. If our hope is in our gold and our investments we'll be worried sick at the present time. We'll be looking for ways of preserving it and protecting it, watching the market, monitoring the news, interpreting events and translating them to our profit. We will be looking to economics for answers and to politics for solutions. We may be astute investors, but I want to remind you of something that I heard when I was a young boy and I never forgot it. In England they publish the contents of people's wills after probate. One day I heard two of my relatives speaking. "Did you know that so-and-so's will was in the paper this morning?" The other one said, "No, how much did he leave?" And the answer was, "Everything." I remember the sheer shock of that answer! One of these days we will all leave *everything*. Then all that will matter will be "an inheritance incorruptible, and undefiled, and that fadeth not away, reserved in heaven for you" (1 Pet. 1:4, *KJV*). Compare the two and hope will well up in your heart. In the fiery trial, hope will grip you and joy will flow like a river.

Hope also comes through a sense of completion. It's understandable that Peter speaks a lot about the end of the age. He knows he is coming to the end of his days, and he's got a feeling that the infant church may be coming to the end of its days too. He still remembers that day on the Mount of Olives when he and others stood looking up into heaven and the angels told them, "This same Jesus, who has been taken from you into heaven, will come back in the same way" (Acts 1:11). The early church expected Him back in their lifetime, and in difficult circumstances they repeated the theme, "Christ will be back soon to establish His glorious kingdom."

Peter still remembers the awful ache in his heart when, on the crucifixion night, he realized the Lord would not establish His kingdom as the disciples expected. The resurrection appearance changed all that and he began to understand that the Kingdom is not an earthly kingdom and that it is going to come at Christ's glorious return. So Peter's heart is full of the thought that He will complete all that He started, and he looks forward to being involved in all that is going to happen.

Recently on a television show I was asked as soon as they opened the telephones, "Do you believe that Jesus is coming again soon?"

"I do not know," I replied.

"You mean to tell me that Jesus isn't coming soon?"

"No, I didn't tell you that Jesus wasn't coming soon. I just told you that I don't know when He is coming. I know He is coming. I know He is coming when He's ready. And I know He will complete all He started when He comes."

The person at the other end of the phone said, "Well, I thought you could have given me something definite on this."

So I said, "I can. His coming is nearer now than it was when we started talking, and that's definite!" We should avoid getting wrapped up in date-picking because He maintains up His divine sleeve that glorious element of surprise. And when He comes with the sound of the trumpet, there may also be a great laugh, and He will say, "Caught you—here I am!" Therein lies our joy.

The Joy That Comes Through Love

What a delightful expression this is in verse 8: "Though you have not seen him, you love him; and even though you do not see him now, you believe in him and are filled with an inexpressible and glorious joy." The inexpressible and glorious joy also comes from our love for Him. What joy it is to love and to demonstrate that love by commitment. Peter loved the Lord Jesus. You can see it in his commitment.

In the Garden of Gethsemane Jesus is praying quietly while Peter is asleep. He had a great gift of sleep! He wakes up—an armed mob has come to get the Lord Jesus! Peter leaps to his feet, whips out his sword and prepares to defend his Lord against the mob. That's commitment! That's love! That's enthusiasm! Peter loves the Lord Jesus.

Shortly thereafter Peter flees back to Galilee convinced he is good for nothing except catching fish. He meets the Lord by the side of the lake. The Lord Jesus makes breakfast, sits down by Peter and says, "Peter, do you love me?" Tentatively Peter responds until, under the gentle, persistent probing of the Lord, he insists vehemently, "Yes, you know I love you!"

The *commitment* of his love showed in the garden with a sword; the *communion* of love showed on the lakeside among the litter of a picnic breakfast as they spent time together. There is no joy like the joy of committed, communing love!

In the land of the free where opportunities for happiness abound there is a sad emptiness in the lives of those who have not found their joy in faith, hope and love—related to Christ.

FOUR

TAKING SALVATION SERIOUSLY
1 Peter 1:10-12

The prophets who predicted in the Old Testament the coming of Messiah, His sufferings and subsequent glories, didn't fully understand all that they were predicting, but they were terribly interested in what was going on. They knew that God was working in their lives, saying something to their contemporaries, but they also recognized that He was speaking to succeeding generations. They recognized that God was speaking about their immediate situation but they also sensed that He was speaking about some ultimate situation. It was clear to them that God was speaking about material things but they also knew that His words, through them, were concerned with eternal issues that had spiritual consequences. There was much that they knew but much more that they didn't know and, because of this, they were deeply interested in what was going on. They searched intently and diligently to find out all they could about the message of salvation that they were prophetically presenting.

Angels are also desperately anxious to look into the whole subject of salvation. The Greek word Peter uses to describe the angels looking down is the same word that was used to describe Peter and John on Resurrection Day as they stooped down to look into the mystery of the empty tomb and the missing body. Angels are stooping down, peering into the earth, looking into the human situation, fascinated with this whole subject of salvation, trying to grasp it, trying to understand it, trying to experience it to the full.

Peter's concern is that, while the prophets are so interested and the angels are so enthralled, so many humans appear indifferent. The prophets only knew a fraction of what humans today know, and the angels recognize that there is no way that they can experience salvation like a human; yet, with all their limitations, both angels and prophets are excited about the whole subject of salvation.

Peter is firmly convinced that the future aspect of salvation is particularly relevant in light of the immediate circumstances in which his readers are living. Let me remind you that Peter talks about salvation in three tenses. In the past tense he can say we have been sprinkled with the blood of Christ; in the present tense he says that we are being sanctified by the Holy Spirit (v. 2). But in the future tense he speaks of the end of our salvation which will be ours at the appearing of Jesus Christ (v. 5). He expects Jesus to return soon. He realizes that Nero may do something crazy and he, Peter, will finish up a martyr. In fact, the Lord Jesus Himself had given a very pointed clue concerning the possibility that Peter's life would be terminated by martyrdom. And for Peter the storm clouds are gathering and it is time to look to the end of all things and the beginning of eternity. Peter knows that his entrance into the future may be accomplished either by death or translation at Jesus Christ's appearing. Either way, to him it is clear that he and his contemporaries should be serious about their salvation.

Peter, in his defense before the Sanhedrin, stated concerning Christ, "Salvation is found in no one else, for there is no other name under heaven given to men by which we must be saved" (Acts 4:12). That's what you call an unequivocal statement, particularly to a hostile congregation. They didn't want to hear it. They didn't want to hear that they *must* be saved, and certainly not that they must be saved through Jesus Christ, and that there is no alternative. It is this unequivocal, three-dimensional, no-nonsense salvation which prophets and angels find so captivating and which apostles preach so fervently. It is this salvation which we cannot afford to ignore or to treat casually.

The Curse of Casualness

Sometimes *casualness is demonstrated by disbelief*. Disbelief is particularly popular in a world where we are blessed scientifically. Scientists have discovered that we are very closely related to the animal kingdom. Because they know our marked similarities they can experiment on animals to learn about human physical and emotional makeup. Unfortunately, this type of beneficial research has led some influential people to conclude that humans are really only sophisticated animals. That may be an insult to animals!

From a biblical point of view we cannot accept that we are just sophisticated animals, because we are spiritual beings of eternal consequence. That is why Peter emphasizes the salvation of our souls. He is interested in our eternal destiny; he is concerned about our unique human spirituality.

The conflict between scientifically-induced (but not proven) theories and biblical principles has led many people to decide for "science" and to disbelieve the Bible, which has led to total casualness regarding the message of salvation. This is the environment in which many of us spend our days, so it is no surprise that disbelief and its attendant casualness to salvation abound. Others don't disbelieve; they are simply disinterested. They say, "Sure I believe I'm a person of eternal significance. Of course there is a God, but frankly I'm not interested. There are far more important things in life for me. When I get old, when I've had my fling, I'll be interested." This casualness is somewhat unnerving, particularly when compared to the prophets who knew only a fraction of what we know and yet were enraptured. The angels who can't experience what we have been offered are leaning out of heaven on tiptoe, excited to see salvation at work on earth.

Then there are those who *demonstrate their casualness by complete disdain*. At a dinner party one evening with a number of surgeons, I heard one of them say, "You amaze me. When it comes to medicine you're brilliant. When it comes to surgery you're superb. But then you sacrifice it all for this Christianity nonsense—I don't understand you."

I said to him, "I don't understand you, because as a scientist you express a total disdain for well-documented areas of human experience without being willing even to consider their validity or scientifically experiment in the area of the spiritual. Your casual approach amazes me!"

Institutions suffer from the sheer curse of casualness too. The educational institution is utterly casual about moral values, eternal issues, spiritual realities. It would root us exclusively in the material and the animal and have us believe that we happened and are drifting, inexorably, towards extinction. Even more worrisome, the church in many instances has become casual about the salvation of people's souls and about their eternal well-being.

Years ago Jill and I were invited to go to the International Congress on World Evangelism in Lausanne, Switzerland. Another ecclesiastical conference was going on at the same time in nearby Geneva. At the congress I spoke to a reporter from one of the Washington newspapers. He said, "You need an ambassador doing Kissinger-style shuttle diplomacy between Lausanne and Geneva. He should help the church decide whether human beings are eternally valid. Many of those guys in Geneva don't believe that there is such a thing as hell. They believe basically in the here and now, so they concentrate on material things, on earthly considerations. But you guys up here believe that people have souls, you believe in heaven, you believe in hell, you believe in salvation. So, of course, you are concerned about the eternal destiny of people. The Christian church must decide what she believes. Do people have souls? Do they have eternal consequence? Is there a heaven? Is there a hell? Is there sin, is there forgiveness, is the cross meaningful, is there salvation or isn't there? Because if there is, get your act together and get serious. And if there isn't, put up the shutters and become a social agency."

It was a sad day for our world when it became necessary to ask the church whether she really believed in the necessity of salvation. But the words of the Washington reporter need to be repeated! The curse of casualness is a compounded curse when it appears in the church.

The curse of casualness comes over in disbelief, in disdain, in disinterest and will produce distance from God. It robs people of reality and life, and banishes them to lostness.

The Strength of Seriousness
We take our salvation seriously because we have a sense of privilege. In comparison to the prophets we know so much; compared to the angels our experience of forgiveness and reconciliation is so great.

Simeon was a godly man, a holy man waiting for the "consolation of Israel"—the arrival of Messiah. It had been revealed to him, as he spent hours and hours trying to understand the Scriptures, that not only would Messiah come, but he, Simeon, would not die until He came. One day a young couple brought their little boy to be circumcised. Simeon was on duty that day and as he looked at the little boy his face lit up; he lifted his head to heaven and said, "Now dismiss your servant in peace. For my eyes have seen your salvation" (Luke 2:29,30). All his life he searched diligently to know what salvation was and, just at the end of his days (he was a very old man), he discovered that salvation was in Jesus Christ. Many people have known this truth since they've known anything—Simeon didn't. What a privilege is ours compared to Simeon's.

John the Baptist was second to none among the prophets, according to Jesus. He spent his time preaching, "Prepare the way for the Lord, make straight paths for him" (Matt. 3:3). People would come to him and say, "Are you the one who shall come?" He said, "No, no, I'm not the one who should come. He will come after me, but He is preferred before me. I'm not even fit to polish His shoes" (see Luke 3). But then he got thrown in prison, had second thoughts and sent a message to Jesus inquiring whether Jesus really was Messiah. John the Baptist didn't have the fullness of truth we have, yet he preached with such intensity that, to silence him, they threw him in jail. Such intensity is remarkable when compared to the relative disinterest shown by those who know far more.

Angels know about the holiness of God in a way that we don't. Their knowledge of the judgment of God, the majesty of God and the sheer power of God is unique; but they don't know what it is like to be saved. They have never been saved; they are servants not sons. They have never known what it is to be so loved that the only Son of God would die on a cross for them. They don't know that, but we do. The angels have vast stores of knowledge and experience but, compared to ours, their knowledge has severe limitations. To look at the angels in this way is to sense our special place of privilege.

My dad was trying to explain salvation to a friend of his, but nothing seemed to make sense. Finally the frustrated friend looked at my dad and said, "Stan, I guess this salvation thing is a bit like

falling in love. It's better felt than telt." The angels
have "telt" it for centuries but never "felt" it for a
second.

   *Salvation should be taken seriously because
there is a great sense of authenticity about it.*
Peter introduces the Holy Spirit in these verses. He
says the prophets were trying to find out the time
and the circumstances to which the Spirit of
Christ in them was pointing. He adds a comment
about those who preach the gospel to you by the
Holy Spirit. He speaks of the ministry of the Holy
Spirit both in the prophets and through the
preachers. He is referring, of course, to the inspiration of Scripture. In his second Epistle he talks
about it again explaining that the prophets didn't
dream up the things they said but were moved
along by the Holy Spirit. Peter's word to describe
the work of the Holy Spirit in inspiration is the
word that describes the wind getting into the sail
of the sailboat, filling it full and sweeping it along.
That's what happened to the prophets.

   If we look at our Bible and say it's just an old
dusty, dry book about a lot of people who lived in
the Middle East thousands of years ago and who
cares, the answer is "nobody cares." But if we
believe that the Word of God was inspired by the
Holy Spirit as the prophets were moved by the
Spirit, then we believe that the Bible is a docu-
ment of eternal significance and the message of
salvation has authenticity. That Peter believed
this with all his heart is evident from his preaching. When he found himself in situations in his
day he related them to what the prophets had said.
On the day of Pentecost the believers were all
jumping around and dancing, filled with the Holy
Spirit. And the onlookers, understandably,

thought they were drunk. But Peter jumped up and said, "Nonsense, they're not drunk. This is what the Prophet Joel spoke about! He, inspired by the Holy Spirit, predicted what is happening today" (see Acts 2).

Peter saw the authenticity of the inspired prophetic message. When he was hauled in front of the authorities he spoke from the Old Testament. He talked about Jesus' resurrection which he insisted the Old Testament predicted. David, the great psalmist, king and prophet, wrote, "Thou wilt not leave my soul in hell, neither suffer thy Holy One to see corruption" (see Ps. 16:10; Acts 2:27). "Do you think David is talking about himself?" Peter asked his hearers. "Of course not. You know where his tomb is. You know he is dead and buried. Open his tomb; his body is corrupt. He's not talking about himself. He is talking about great David's greatest Son." What an authentic word we have in Scripture! When we sense our privilege and accept the Bible's authenticity we will become serious about both salvation and Scripture.

The apostle said that the Spirit preached through the preachers who were responsible for founding the churches of Asia Minor. They were not ragtag and bobtail refugees who came along and told fantasy stories. They were people inspired by the Holy Spirit. And as they spoke there was a touch of authenticity about them and their message. The combination of Spirit-inspired Word, Spirit-anointed preaching, Spirit-aided hearing and Spirit-prompted response produces an authentic experience of God that must be taken seriously.

Seriousness also comes through a sense of

wonder. Familiarity, they tell me, breeds contempt. "Tell me the old, old story and bore me out of my skull one more time" is the attitude of many a person in a pew. They go to be bored with great regularity, with tremendous devotion to duty, rather like visiting the dentist. I don't understand how they can hear the Word of God and lose a sense of wonder. Let me just show you why the Word of God is so wonderful. The prophets spoke of "the grace that was to come" (1 Pet. 1:10). Grace is God choosing to give us what we don't deserve for no other reason than He chose to do it. All that we are, all that we have, all that we ever hope to be, we are and have and hope to be because of the grace of God. It's wonderful; but if we lose our sense of wonder, we'll lose our sense of seriousness.

Christ's suffering also leads to this sense of wonder. The inspired prophets were pointing to the sufferings of Christ. If we sit at Peter's feet for a few minutes we will hear repeatedly the message of the wonders of God's grace and the immensity of Christ's suffering. I may lose my sense of wonder about the sufferings of Christ, but Peter never did. Perhaps he never forgot because his behavior had so intensified those sufferings. Christ's sufferings weren't just physical. Did you ever think of the horror of the sinless One being made sin, the eternal One suddenly being separated from the eternal Father and crying from the depths of His soul, "My God, my God, why have you forsaken me?" Did you ever try to imagine the sufferings of Christ when He looked at His disciples as they forsook Him and fled, and Peter, the one who promised to be there, running away, crying, from a little girl?

It is easy to sing, "When I survey the wondrous cross on which the Prince of Glory died, my richest gain I count but loss and pour contempt on all my pride." But if I can survey the wondrous cross and lose the wonder, I've got a severe spiritual problem caused probably by some hard core of resistance, some deep-seated sin that is stopping my ears to the sheer wonder of the message of Christ.

Peter also talks about the wonder of the glories that would follow Christ's suffering and death. He was referring to the glorious Resurrection, the glorious ascension and the glories of the coming Kingdom. All these subjects, he insists, were taught by the prophets. The contemporaries of Christ thought the Old Testament was teaching that the Kingdom would be on earth, that the blessing would be material and that the Messiah would be a great military conqueror who would get the Romans off their backs. They were excited about this.

But Peter had learned that the truth was even more exciting. The kingdom is not earthly, it's heavenly; the blessing is not material, it's spiritual; He isn't getting the Romans off our back, He's getting Satan off our back! He is saying if those people in the Old Testament had a sense of wonder, how much more should we? Prophets, angels and Old Testament saints with limited knowledge and experience, compared to believers in the present age, were serious about God's salvation. Peter's point is clear—we should be careful not to be casual about matters which others regard as crucial.

FIVE

BE HOLY
1 Peter 1:13-16

Whenever I find the word *therefore* in Scripture I ask myself, "What's it there for?" The answer, of course, is the word *therefore* is there to link what is gone with what is coming. Almost invariably in Scripture you will find that "what is gone" is a doctrinal statement and "what is coming" is a practical application. In the early part of the Epistle the Apostle Peter has been outlining the Christian message of salvation, but now he is concerned about the practical application of this message.

The unequivocal statement of the apostle is that believers are to "be holy." It would be true to say that all the ethical demands of God are wrapped up in this call to holiness in the same way that all the attributes of God are contained in His holiness. It is very unfortunate, therefore, that holiness is a subject that makes a lot of believers very nervous. Some sections of the church never mention it. They have worked out an ecclesiastical system where holiness is not terribly necessary. Other segments of the church recognize that there has to be a relationship with Jesus Christ based on repentance and faith. They insist, therefore, that people don't just join and show up spasmodically but that they testify to the fact that they have been saved and that they are looking forward to going to heaven when they die. But that's about all that is expected of them.

Some areas of the church recognize that neither of these two approaches is adequate because they sense that something has to be done, in terms of practical living, in between the experience of being saved and the ultimate experience of going to be with the Lord. So they put great emphasis upon the practicalities of a life of holiness. They vary in their theological terminology and they emphasize different experiences. Accordingly, they are regarded with some degree of suspicion by other believers and, in order to maintain their position, they have become somewhat strident in their protestations and extreme in their positions. They are resented by others and accused of projecting a "holier-than-thou" attitude. It is unfortunate that "holier than thou" has become a derogatory term and "holiness" a bone of contention among believers.

As there is all this confusion, reticence, and division in the church on the subject of holiness, it's hardly surprising that the subject is largely neglected. It is equally no surprise that there is considerable confusion on the subject outside the church. Some of the worst epithets reserved for believers by nonbelievers are "Holy Joe" and "Holy Roller." In their eyes a believer who says nothing and does nothing is fine, but a believer who tries to apply and promote his faith is to be rejected and ridiculed. It is interesting to note that *holy* (in some form) is the term they use. So the whole subject of holiness is one fraught with difficulty, for people both inside and outside the church. However, Scripture does say, "Be holy, says the Lord, because I am holy"; so notwithstanding the difficulties, the confusion, the considerable reticence on the part of many of God's people we must try to deal with this subject of "being holy."

Holiness Defined

The original meaning of the ancient biblical word translated *holy* is "to be separated" or "to be cut off" and, accordingly, "to be different" and "to be distinct." God has chosen this word *holy* to describe Himself. He quite definitely states that "holy" is His name. When God attributes the name *holy* to Himself (and, incidentally, the expression "as he who called you is holy" in verse 15 can just as well mean "Holy [that is His name] is the one who called you") He is drawing attention to the fact that He is separate, different, distinct, transcendent; He is "totally other." This is the special meaning that begins to appear in Scripture concerning the word *holy*. It relates to God Himself.

You'll remember, for instance, in Isaiah 6 that the prophet had a vision of heaven in which he saw the throne room, the Holy One sitting on the throne and the angelic beings singing, "Holy, holy, holy is the Lord Almighty" (v. 3), etc. You remember also that when Joshua was speaking to his people and asking them to get their act together he said, "Choose whom you are going to serve. Stop stumbling and being unsure of where you are going to go. As for me and for my house we will serve the Lord." They replied, "We'll serve the Lord." He said, "You can't serve the Lord, He's Holy." (See Josh. 24:15-19.) In other words they were very flippant, they were very casual about their response. He said, "You don't even know who He is. You haven't grasped His otherness, His transcendence, His distinctiveness. You haven't begun to understand that to serve the Lord means to recognize that He is so totally different that all you are and all you have and all you do is going to have to be totally different. It doesn't just mean to be different or 'other,' but it means to be different or distinct, as God is different and distinct."

Then we move into a further development of the word and we begin to see a practical meaning. If God is Holy, that which is identified with Him is called holy. The earliest illustration of this is in Genesis 2:3 where the Lord, having worked for six days and created all things, rested and declared the seventh day "holy." It doesn't mean that it had a special character of itself. It had just 24 hours like any other day, it had 60 minutes to every hour, it had a sunrise in the east and a normal sunset in the west. The only different thing about it was that now it was the Lord's day. It had been set apart specifically for Him and, accordingly, it was different or holy. (Incidentally, that's how we first got our word *holiday*. Holidays used to be *holy-days*.) As we develop this idea in Scripture we see that not only days and things are set aside for the Holy One but also people are set apart and are called a holy people. This, of course, is one of the powerful statements that Peter makes further on in his Epistle—that Christians are holy people. That is, they have chosen to identify with the Holy One; therefore they are regarded as being different, separate, distinct people.

This brings us to the ethical meaning of the word. If holy people are to be clearly distinguishable, they must exhibit distinctive life-styles based on different ethical considerations derived from the Holy One. God—the Holy One—says what ought to be done because He is the one who decides what is right and what is wrong and He is the source of all morality and ethics. In short, once a believer sees that he is a holy person identified with the Holy One, required to live a holy life based on a holy ethic, he will begin to understand what it means to be holy.

This idea can be seen clearly in the Old Testament, but with a certain ceremonial emphasis. For example, in Leviticus 19 God says to His people, "I'm holy; therefore be ye holy" (see v. 1). And He promptly gives them instructions, some of which seem very funny to us at the present time. He forbade them to wear a garment made up of two kinds of material. That sounds absolutely ludicrous to us; but think about it for a minute. If they had a garment made up of two kinds of material, it meant that they used the material that was available in their own land but mixed it with material from elsewhere. By so doing, they were mixing that which stood for the Lord and that which was opposed to the Lord. It seems a small thing to us but in the ceremonial it was very important. The clothes they wore were to thereby demonstrate the fact that they were totally identified with the Lord, His land, and that which His land produced. If they could not manage on the Lord's provision they didn't want anything to do with anything else. They were separate. They were distinct. They were other. They were people set apart. They were a holy people. And so the ceremonial law developed.

When we get into the New Testament we'll discover that the emphasis switched from outward ceremony to an emphasis on the change of heart attitude. In the Old Testament the difference was seen by their externals, to a very large extent; but in the New Testament there was a tremendous emphasis on an internal heart transformation. New Testament holiness in the heart would produce holy people who would begin to desire what the Holy One desires and who would act upon what the Holy One was acting upon.

Holiness Desired

In many hearts there is no great desire to be holy. People want to be saved, to go to heaven, to be happy, to be healthy, to be wealthy, and some don't even mind being wise, but who needs holiness!? So let's ask ourselves, What are the factors that would motivate towards holiness? There are five that I can identify in this passage.

The first one is the character of God. God says on numerous occasions, and Peter quotes from the Old Testament, "Be holy, because I am holy" (1 Pet. 1:16). We may be tempted to say to God, "God, why did you tell me to be holy?" The answer is very simple. "Because I am." The greatest motivational factor towards holiness for the believer ought to be the character of God. God revealed Himself to us, we liked what we saw, and we made a very simple decision. Nobody held a gun to our heads—we freely decided to be the Lord's. Those who freely choose to identify with the Lord must remember, continually, who the Lord is—the Holy One. We must be reasonable and recognize that there is something most attractive about His holiness. Otherwise we wouldn't have been foolish enough to identify with Him. In other words, the very character of God which drew us to Him is holiness and, therefore, if holiness is so attractive how can we be against it in our own lives?

The second thing that motivates us toward holiness is the call of God. You notice that Peter says, "As he who called you is holy, so be holy." God doesn't just want to give us things; He wants us to be part of all that He is. He called us to a relationship. He called us to Himself. He so loves the Lord Jesus that He wants a lot more like Him. Christ is the firstborn of many brethren and He called us to be with Him and ultimately like Him. This was His call and it was to this call that we responded. Now, of course, sometimes we'd like very much to respond to His call on our terms, not His.

My youngest son, Pete, grew a beard in high school. He was going out for the basketball team and he was obviously going to make the team. He worked through the summer and the practice sessions, and then the big day arrived when the cuts were coming—and he survived all the cuts. One day a photographer came to take a picture of the varsity basketball team of which Pete was a member. At the last minute he was told to sit on the side. When he asked the coach why he wasn't included in the picture he was told, "We don't want any hairy monsters in our picture." The coach added, "If you want to play on this team you get rid of that beard, and if you want the beard you don't play on this team. It's as simple as that." Pete didn't have any problem at all. He came home and said, "Dad, what must I do to be shaved!"

I suppose Pete could have mirrored the present age and said, "If I want to grow a beard I can grow a beard. I also feel I'm being discriminated against, and I'm going to get an attorney who will protect my constitutional rights, and I'm going to kick up a stink and I'll get this whole athletic program closed." But he didn't. He understood that if he wanted to be on the team, this was his coach who knew what he was doing, and Pete was going to play it his way. He shaved off his beard and played very happily for him ever after.

God said, "Listen, if you're going to play on my team, be holy. I'm holy, and that's how it is; if you don't want to be holy, don't join my team. I called you to holiness."

The third factor in holiness is God's command. If God's character and call isn't enough for you then how about God's command? A good friend of mine recently said to me, "I get so confused about the whole subject of prayer I just say to myself, 'Well why bother doing it?'"

So I answered, "It's easy to answer that one and I appreciate easy questions because I usually get hard ones."

He asked, "What's easy about that question?"

I said, "The easy answer to the question is you pray because He told you to." It's the same way with holiness. We may not understand holiness, we may not appreciate holiness, we may not even like holiness but that's all delightfully irrelevant, because He told us to be holy anyway!

The fourth factor is the consistency of God. Holiness is not something that God has recently sprung on us. You'll notice that Peter says, "As it is written, be holy for I am holy." He is pointing out that throughout the Old Testament God has revealed Himself as holy, making holy demands upon His people, giving them means of being holy. He has shown them the advantages of holiness and He has also shown them the consequences if they refuse to be holy. He has had one basic, fundamental message right down through His dealings with humanity. The consistency of God is such that nobody can ever say, "I didn't know I was supposed to be holy. This is the small print on the bottom of the policy." We can't say that kind of thing if we've even begun to start thinking through who God is and what He has consistently been saying.

Then we need to be holy because it is the choice of God. Notice the word *therefore* (v. 13) links the passage we're talking about with the previous verses which describe the salvation that is available to us. The apostle reminds us that in the light of God's choice of us to come into His salvation we must always remember that the salvation He chose for us to enjoy includes holiness.

Lee Iacocca told the people at Chrysler, who were resisting a proposed wage freeze, "Good jobs at $17.50 per hour we have in plenty. Jobs at $20.00 per hour we don't have. It's as simple as that." The chairman of the board had decided and made his position very clear. At the risk of confusing God with Lee Iacocca and the purposes of God with Chrysler Motor Corporation, workers at Chrysler and servants of God have this in common—their choices are limited by the choices of those in charge. The choice of God, the consistency, the command and the character of God all point to the necessity for holiness.

We must also talk about the factors which militate against holiness. They are an unholy trinity—

the world, the flesh, and the devil. *The devil* rebelled against the Father and has not stopped rebelling against Him since that time. He is utterly and totally opposed to all the Father is and all the Father stands for. He is against the Holy One; therefore, you can be sure he is dead set against holiness.

Not only that, we recognize that *the world* crucified the Son. Somebody asked me the other day, "If Jesus came back today would they crucify Him?" I said, "No, it's illegal, but they would find another way of getting rid of Him." The world and its system has always been fundamentally opposed to all that Christ represents, and as we live our lives in this world we must reckon with secular hostility to holy aspirations.

In addition, we have within us *the flesh*, which the Scriptures say fights against the Spirit. We have to recognize that we live our lives with the devil over us, the world around us and the flesh within us. When it comes to holiness we have a lot against us.

Holiness Developed

On the one hand Scripture says that holiness is a position that is ours the moment we become Christ's, but on the other hand holiness is seen as a progressive development in our lives. When we talk about holiness being developed we're talking about that ongoing growth of a life that is distinctive and different and separated unto God. There are two major ingredients to this: first, the divine ingredient and second, the human ingredients.

The divine ingredient of holiness is the ministry of the Holy Spirit. But Peter does not emphasize this. We will remind ourselves that there is a sanctifying (making holy) work of the Holy Spirit. He alerts us, for instance, to who the Father is, thus introducing us to ideas of holiness. He also points out to us the unholiness of the evil one, the world around us, and the flesh within us. This Instructor brings conviction and concern, aspirations and longings; and, of course, He is also the dynamic power without which holy aspirations would become unholy frustrations.

The first of the human ingredients is a well-ordered mind, as is clear from Peter's instruction, "Therefore, prepare your minds for action" (1 Pet. 1:13). Literally, "gird up the loins of your mind." You remember that one day Peter was fishing. He had taken off his outer robe; then he saw the Lord Jesus standing on the bank so he put on his robe and jumped into the water. It's difficult to run in the water at any time but it's impossible in Eastern robes! So he bent down, got hold of the hem and pulled it up between his legs and tucked the ends into his belt. He girded up his loins! When it comes to holiness we've got a whole lot of extraneous matter in our minds and we must recognize what's a hindrance and get rid of it. This means doing some good, solid thinking about the Holy One, and guarding our minds from contrary influences.

Later in this passage of Scripture Peter talks about living in ignorance, but that is not a problem for those whose minds have been enlightened by God. But believers may have an untidy mind or a desperately unexercised mind concerning the Lord.

The second human ingredient is a well-disciplined life. King James uses the word "sober," which, unfortunately, has limited connotations.

For many it means "don't get drunk" or "to go around with a long face," or both of the above. *New International Version* says to "be self-controlled." This is a better translation, particularly in light of the unholy trinity's activity which is so ferociously opposed to holy living. God has outlined His limits for us—which are not to spoil our fun, but to enrich our lives. There are certain things that God is against because God is holy. There are certain things that He is for, for the same reason. To identify with Christ means we are against what He is against and for what He is for. Once this is understood we begin to gladly accept and appreciate His limits and live with self-control within them. This is how we begin to develop holiness. It comes from a well-ordered mind and a well-disciplined life.

A well-defined goal is the third human ingredient in holiness. Peter says, "Set your hope fully on the grace to be given you when Jesus Christ is revealed." The goal of the Christian is to live and move toward the day when the Lord Jesus Christ will come again and receive to Himself those who have committed themselves to Him. He will take us to be with Him, usher us into the presence of His Father. And when we see Him we will be like Him and will live for all eternity in the full flow of our redeemed humanity, glorified in the presence of the Father—that's quite a goal! Once we get our minds well-ordered, our lives well-disciplined and our goals well-defined, we will find one theme running through the whole of our lives—holiness, holiness, holiness. It's rather obvious that if our goal is to be with Him and like Him then, in the interim, we're going to want to be more and more like Him because we're looking forward more and more to being with Him. Now if we say we love the Lord but we don't want to be like Him—we're a living contradiction.

The fourth human ingredient is a well-established conversion. The apostle adds, "Do not conform to the evil desires you had when you lived in ignorance." Peter calls Christians "obedient children," but Paul, writing to the believers in Ephesus said, "You are children of disobedience" (see Eph. 2:2, *KJV*). This is a monumental change of status. Before converting to Christ we wanted to be disobedient; now we want to be obedient. That's one way we can tell if we're converted or not. We don't have to look for a dramatic experience so much as a change of attitude; not only that, a change of understanding. We used to live in ignorance, but now we have begun to understand. Then there is a change of desire. Before we just had evil desires to do our own thing, our own way, to be our own person, indulge our own passions; but now we're done with all that.

To be holy, then, is not to be stale and sterile but rather to be refreshingly, distinctly different. Not the bizarre difference of eccentricity or the contrived self-conscious difference of faddism, but the difference that comes from a heart in tune with a refreshingly different God. In tough times the world needs this kind of holiness.

SIX

A SENSE OF VALUES
1 Peter 1:17-25

The Circus Maximus in the Rome of Peter's day was big enough to contain half as many people again as the Rose Bowl in Pasadena; and shortly after Peter's time it was enlarged to hold a quarter of a million people. The streets, temples and palaces thronged with people from every corner of the globe. All roads in those days led to Rome. It was a remarkable city, the center of a vast empire; yet Peter appears to be decidedly underwhelmed about this empire and all its vast glories and achievements.

Nero, the emperor at that time, whose awesome powers when married to his bizarre brutality made him a fearsome opponent, apparently held no great terror for Peter. Peter knew what the Lord had told him about his own death, and he probably sensed that he didn't have long to go, and yet he was not at all terrified by Nero. He was neither overwhelmed by the glory and the majesty of the empire, nor threatened by the power and fury of the emperor; and he didn't want the Christians to be either. Peter's approach to life and death, power and glory, pain and suffering, success and failure was governed by a special set of values which he endeavored to teach the believers in the Roman provinces.

Notice several important things concerning values.

Certain Things Must Be Underlined

External appearances are deceptive. Verse 17 states: "You call on a Father who judges each man's work impartially." The word translated "impartially" here is related to the Greek word for *mask.* In other words, God is not fooled by the masks we wear, or misled by the makeup we put on. He is not particularly affected by the actions we go through or the acting we engage in. He does not look on the outside but the inside.

When Samuel was sent to find a king for Israel God warned him not to judge as man judges. Peter learned this lesson the hard way. One day he was having his quiet time on the roof—it was a very quiet time. He'd gone to sleep and God was not able to communicate with him through his Bible or his study notes so He got through to him by a vision. The vision had a great sheet, full of all kinds of animals, let down in front of Peter's eyes. The Lord said to Peter, "Get up, Peter. Kill and eat."

Peter was horrified that the Lord apparently didn't understand about kosher laws and he said, "I could never do that!"

The Lord replied, "Don't you ever dare call unclean what I have called clean."

Peter probably didn't know what was happening until some Gentiles arrived at his front door and asked him to accompany them to the home of a Roman centurion called Cornelius. Up until that time Peter had no dealings with Gentiles. He would never enter a Gentile home because it would be unclean to him. But God was saying to him in the vision, "Don't evaluate by externals, Peter. You've got to understand that I'm reading the heart of this man." When Peter arrived in Cornelius's home and preached, the Holy Spirit fell upon those assembled, and Peter said, "Now I see that God is no respecter of persons." (See Acts 10.) The fact that he uses a similar expression in the Epistle shows that he had learned that you can make some bad mistakes on the basis of external evaluations.

Financial resources are perishable. Peter calls "silver and gold" perishable things. He is talking particularly about silver and gold coins. Precious metals obviously fluctuate in real value, and inflation can play havoc with wealth. But more importantly, Peter says that silver and gold coins have negligible redemptive value. Unfortunately, in our society at the present time we don't have a very healthy sense of values because we tend to think that financial resources are the answer to all our problems. Peter is pointing out that these values are severely limited and need to be treated as such.

Traditional norms are suspect. He goes on to talk about "the empty way of life handed down to you from your forefathers." This is a very striking thing for Peter to say because as a convinced, conservative, orthodox Jew he was very proud of the traditions of his forefathers. The problem was, however, that he had to learn that sometimes forefathers were dead wrong. No doubt they were well-meaning men. Often they had introduced things intended to assist in the search for deeper values. But as the years went by their descendants forgot that the aids were intended to be aids and they began to substitute the aid for the end, the ritual for the reality. Vanity is pervading all that we are, and if we become locked into our traditions and feel that they are of paramount importance we may be utterly misled by them.

The Lord Jesus taught Peter a lot in this regard. I think of one instance when He was at the Feast of Tabernacles. The high priest carried a pitcher down the steep incline to the spring of Gihon, stooped down and filled the pitcher. Then he returned up to the Temple area with the holiday crowds following him. Standing in a prominent place the priest poured out the water in a solemn ceremony related to the commemoration of the hard days of wilderness living which God had enabled His people to survive. This ritual had gone on for centuries and no doubt had lost its significance for many of the spectators.

The Lord Jesus, watching the water ceremony, stood up at that crucial moment and shouted, "If a man is thirsty, let him come to me and drink. Whoever believes in me . . . streams of living water will flow from within him" (John 7:37,38). You see, Jesus was saying, "Your ritual and your traditions which came from your forefathers point to me. I am the source of living water, but you're so wrapped up with your cultural traditions that you've forgotten the truth. You have substituted the ritual for the reality and you are putting trust in tradition."

Temporal issues are transient. There are two very interesting phrases in verse 20. Speaking of the Lord Jesus, Peter says, "He was chosen before the creation of the world, but was revealed in these last times." When we put the expressions "before the creation of the world" and "these last times" together we generate a tremendous sense of time in opposition to eternity. We do not know how or when the worlds were made, but by faith we believe they were created by the Word of God. He, of course, existed before the creation, living in a state of continuous existence. When He chose to make time He created something entirely new. He determined that time would not go on indefinitely; there would be an end to time and He would introduce before the end what the Bible calls "the last times." When we understand this we realize eternity, but we are terribly transient creatures of time. Therefore, if we're going to have a right sense of values we dare not operate purely on the basis of temporal values. We must always think in terms of eternal values. Life is part of creation, time is part of creation, today is part of the last times and soon time will be through and we will be ushered into eternity to face the God who, before creation, already existed in eternal existence.

Spiritual experiences are confusing. The apostle says in verse 23, "You have been born again, not of perishable seed, but of imperishable, through the living and enduring word of God." The Word of God, when sown in people's hearts, brings forth life eternal, is imperishable. But there is perishable seed that is not the truth which, when sown in people's hearts, brings untold confusion to bear. This is important because we need to remember that all spiritual experiences are not necessarily valid. It is possible, for instance, for there to be a pseudo conversion which is nothing

more than a change of heart, or a change of life-
style. People may give up unwholesome activities
and begin to be better people; but this should
never be confused with the miracle of regeneration
that comes through the Holy Spirit germinating
the seed of the Word of God sown in people's lives.
There is a considerable propagation of the truth of
the gospel but at the present time there is also a
disconcerting proliferation of misinformation.

Recently I was reluctantly invited to appear on
a TV show in Milwaukee. The producers didn't
really want me because they said, "He's just a pastor who will talk about Christianity, and who
needs that?" However, these same producers
arranged for an astrologer to make a daily appearance on that show because they regarded his con-
tribution as more valid and realistic! We must be
careful to recognize the seed being sown and the
fruit being grown.

Mortal men are finite. Quoting Isaiah, Peter
says, "All men are like grass and all their glory is
like the flowers of the field; the grass withers and
the flowers fall, but the word of the Lord stands
forever" (1 Pet. 1:24,25). When we get into trouble
we promptly look to a man to deliver us. We pin
our hopes on him, but if he doesn't deliver we get
rid of him and get another man on whom to pin a
whole new set of hopes. There is no question that
some grasses are more impressive than others.
Since Peter expected Nero to do something crazy at
any moment, he had no option but to recognize
that Nero had awesome power. He was pretty significant, but he was, in Peter's estimation, only
significant grass. We must get mortal man in perspective. He comes out of nowhere, he shoots up,
and he grows into significance, but soon he is

gone, and the world will go on without him. Therefore, a real system of values recognizes that mortal
man is finite, that even mighty man is limited.

Cultural glories are ephemeral. Not only are
men like grass but "all their glory is like the
flowers of the field." Peter had seen the Circus
Maximus, had visited the Forum and seen where
Nero was building his artificial lakes. He understood that the emperor had plans to build a golden
palace. He had traveled the roads the Romans had
built, had seen their empire and benefited from
their laws; but he insisted that even such glory
would pass away. We sometimes have a hard time
believing what Peter believed because our values
are rooted in our culture. We know that other cultures have failed. Some of us have traveled around
the world and we've seen the relics and the rem-
nants of previous majestic cultures. We will admit
that previous cultures had the seeds of their
destruction sown in their foundation, but we
believe that ours is different. Ours will be the first
one that will survive. It will never become corrupt
and never will decay and never will become like the
flowers that are glorious but inevitably fall off the
tree. We may deny that we feel this about our culture, but our identification with it is a clearer indication of our attitude towards it than our protestations.

If we're going to get our values right we must
not forget these things.

Certain Things Need to Be Understood

I want you to notice what Peter says about the
Fatherhood of God, the Saviourhood of Christ,
and the brotherhood of believers.

The Fatherhood of God.

God is the Father who judges impartially, according to verse 17. Our society is quite open to hear about God—provided He is innocuous and primarily committed to our well-being. But if we begin to talk in terms of a Father who judges all men's work impartially, a certain degree of discomfort becomes evident. Yet the clear teaching of Scripture is that all we have done and all that we are will come under the scrutiny of the eternal Father who will function as our judge.

But there is another side of the coin. We not only have a Father who is a Judge but we have a Judge who is our Father. That helps a lot. To know that our lives will be brought under the scrutiny of the One who has offered to adopt us into His family is to add a fundamental concept to our value system.

He is the Father who hears compassionately. Peter, when he wrote, "You call on the Father," uses the word Paul used when he stood trial and said, "I appeal to Caesar," and the response was immediate—"To Caesar you will go" (Acts 25:11,12). Any Roman appealing to Caesar was guaranteed a hearing, but more importantly any believer "calling" on the Father has His full attention. He is committed to hearing us compassionately. When the going gets tough we should concentrate not on ephemeral values, mortal man, financial resources or external appearances, but on the Fatherhood of God, because He will judge impartially and always be committed to hearing us compassionately.

He is also the Father who redeems eternally. In 1 Peter 1:19 we are told what God has done through "the precious blood of Christ, a lamb without blemish or defect." The word *redeemer* is related to *ransom* and emphasizes the price of salvation. There is a sense in which our salvation is free, but that does not mean it is without cost. In the same way that the first law of economics states, "There is no free lunch," the first law of redemption is that free salvation cost the Father everything. The glorious truth of the gospel proclaims that He chose to pay it.

He is the Father who plans sovereignly. Peter wrote, "He [Christ] was chosen before the creation of the world" (v. 20). Some people believe that God had Plan A and Plan B. Plan A was that the Garden of Eden would be great, that He would make man and give him woman and they would live happily ever after, and everybody would enjoy everybody. Then unfortunately Plan A came apart at the seams, so God put Plan B into operation. He sent Jesus, had Him die on the cross and then took Him back to heaven. However popular this idea may be, it does not agree with Scripture.

Before the foundation of the world God had already ordained that Jesus should be the Lamb without defect and without blemish and would die and take away the sins of the world. If we look at it from a human point of view we struggle with this truth. I have heard people say, "You mean to tell me that God made man knowing what man would do, but made us anyway, let us do wrong knowing He already had the answer? That's weird!" It is weird. It is one of the great sublime mysteries of the sovereign God. But when the going gets tough it is wonderful to realize that you can trust in a Father who had the end of all things planned before the beginning!

He is also the Father who triumphed glori-

ously. Verse 21 goes on to say, "Through him you believe in God, who raised him from the dead and glorified him." What else did God do? He raised up Christ from the dead, took Him to His own right hand, gave Him great glory, seated Him there and told Him to wait until His enemies be made His footstool. He has triumphed over sin, death, hell, and all evil, and He is totally committed to making all His enemies His footstool and, ultimately, He will be revealed on a cosmic, eternal scale as the One who is "all in all"! He has triumphed gloriously—this is the Father.

When the going gets tough, one thing won't come apart and won't slip through your fingers, and that is the Father. This is the bedrock truth upon which we build.

The Saviourhood of Christ.

We need to recognize the *substitutionary aspect of the Saviourhood of Christ.* Peter, drawing from the rich heritage of the Old Testament, thinks of the Passover Lamb which was carefully nurtured and scrutinized, to make sure that it was without defect, before being offered for the sins of the people. In this ancient ritual he sees a picture of the Lord Jesus, who for 33 years was scrutinized and criticized and seen to be without defect. He was shown to be the spotless Son of God who voluntarily died as a substitute, like the lamb in the Old Testament. Innocent, blameless, without blemish, the lamb dies on behalf of the people that their sins might be forgiven; so Christ, blameless, died not for His sin but died as a substitute for the sins of the world; He died that we might be saved.

Then there is the *saving aspect of the*

Saviourhood of Christ. The word *redeemed* in the phrase means "to release by paying a ransom." When the Iranians held the 52 American hostages, they asked for 24 billion dollars ransom. There was a long standoff and deadlock at this point, the result being that they didn't get the money and we didn't get the hostages. If the Lord Jesus Christ had not laid down His life as a ransom for billions of people, the standoff would have been understandable but the ransom was paid and the deliverance secured.

The Brotherhood of Believers.

The apostle makes a strong statement in verses 22 and 23 concerning the behavior of the believers: "Now that you have purified yourselves by obeying the truth so that you have sincere love for your brothers, love one another deeply, from the heart. For you have been born again." The sheer value of the community of believers must never be overlooked. Sometimes the relationship of believer to believer is similar to the relationship of pool balls to pool tables. We all have our identity—our own little colors, and we all sit on the same table. Often we're propelled around the fellowship; we ricochet off the cushions and bang into each other. But as soon as we touch, we use the momentum of our collision to head us off in opposite directions again. This goes on until someone slips off into the pocket and we give him a good funeral and say nice things about his life of colorful collision. Perhaps we need to recognize how vital is the brotherhood of believers to our spiritual experience. I am sure Peter places this truth alongside the Fatherhood of God and the Saviourhood of Christ to highlight dramatically the significance of the brotherhood.

We all appeal to the same Father; we have all been "born of the same seed." We have all "purified ourselves by obeying the truth." In other words we enjoy the same life; we accept the same truth which we seek to obey because we know the same Father through the same Son. Because we have all these things in common we share the same love, we love the same truth, we love the same Father and Son and we experience the same redemption. It is in the community of this unity that there is strength. These are the values we build on if we are to live adequately when the going gets tough.

Certain Tasks Must Be Undertaken

The first task in value building is the *development of a reverent life-style*. "Since you call on a Father who judges each man's work impartially, live your lives as strangers here in reverent fear" (v. 17). To develop a reverent life-style means to fear doing damage to the life of the brotherhood, the reputation of the Father, or the gospel of the Son. It also means that we should become decidedly irreverent about many things that a lot of other people revere. How often we revere a lot of empty, useless tradition! How often we treat with tremendous solemnity that which is really hilarious. It seems that sometimes we're remarkably casual about the Father, the Son and the fellowship, and deeply in awe of things that have little intrinsic value and no lasting significance.

The second task is the *development of a confident attitude*. Peter, having outlined what the Father has done through the Son, reminds us that our faith and hope should be in God (v. 21). Christians should be incorrigibly confident. Self-confidence is not what Peter had in mind. He had been an expert in that field for a number of years and had proved how misplaced is that kind of confidence. Since coming to know the One of whom he writes in his Epistle, his own basis of confidence had been altered as thoroughly as the results of this change had been demonstrated dramatically. He wishes nothing less for all believers.

The third task is *developing a fervent relationship!* "Now that you have purified yourselves by obeying the truth so that you have sincere love for your brothers, love one another deeply, from the heart" (v. 22). The building of relationships, like the construction of anything of value, takes time and effort. But the caliber of relationship of which Peter speaks demands a fervency of spirit which will be as demanding as the results of such fellowship will be rewarding. Only those who commit themselves to such a task will know the resources of God available for troubled people in tough times.

SEVEN

SPIRITUAL GROWTH
1 Peter 2:1-3

Toughness and tension are related. When I injured a leg running, the muscles deteriorated until it was necessary for me to go through a series of isometric exercises which, through tension, would build up the muscles. In the same way, tense times make tough believers. It is also true that tense times require mature behavior from believers, and Peter, knowing this, addresses the subject of spiritual growth towards maturity.

The Initiation of Spiritual Growth

There are four things that Peter mentions which are related to the initiation of spiritual growth.

First, the proclamation of the Word of God. The previous chapter of the Epistle concluded with "the word of the Lord stands forever. . . . And this is the word that was preached to you." This Word of God is like a seed which, when planted in the warm, fertile soil of a receptive heart, brings forth life. Sometimes when we listen to the Word of God we behave as if we were evaluating the Word of God; but that's like saying that soil evaluates the seed. When we put seed in soil, the seed evaluates the soil. This is the thrust of the Parable of the Sower with which Peter was no doubt familiar.

The people in the Roman provinces had shown themselves receptive to the Word and had made a good start in their spiritual life and growth, reminding us that there is no substitute in spiritual experience for the proclamation of and response to the seed of the Word of God.

Second, the introduction to the Son of God. There is a simple instruction in Psalm 34:8 which says, "Taste and see that the Lord is good." Presumably Peter was thinking of this when he told his readers, "You have tasted that the Lord is good." Now when the Word of God is presented it is rather like a meal being placed on the table. It is not enough to be told by way of proclamation, "This is good!" The real benefit comes from tasting. When we receive a presentation of the Lord Jesus we are required to trust Him and we're required to obey Him. As we do this we "taste of Him" and we come into the good of all that He has promised. We begin to discover the reality of His forgiveness, the sheer love that He has for us, and His power in our lives. In other words, we are introduced to the Lord and we taste and see that He is good.

Third, the reception of the life of God. In his first Epistle Peter says, "We have been born again," and in the second Epistle he says we "participate in the divine nature." Both expressions point to the fact that we experience the indwelling presence of the Lord Jesus who died and rose again for us. By the proclamation of the Word of God we are initiated into all that God has to teach us. In our introduction to the Son of God, we're initiated into a divine/human relationship, and through the reception of the life of God we are introduced to the possibilities of a totally new life, lived in the power of His indwelling presence.

Fourth, the recognition of the people of God. In England if somebody got a little arrogant we used to say to them, "Remember, you're not the only pebble on the beach." Sometimes in our spiritual experience we act as if we are the only person related to the Lord. But we must remember that God is bringing thousands of people to Himself. All these "born ones" have the same Father, acknowledge the same Son, are indwelt by the same Spirit, enjoy the same life and are related to each other as well as being related to the Father, Son and Holy Spirit. If we have come into an experience of the truth as it is in the Lord Jesus, we come into an experience of all the other people who are experiencing the truth too. That is why Peter calls us "brothers" and insists that "sincere love" characterize the relationship. Like infants placed in a family so that they might be raised, the spiritual infant is placed among more mature believers, called the family of God, that through that relationship they may grow up into Christ.

The Stimulation of Spiritual Growth

There is a driving, craving force about a body that is hungry. Peter uses the analogy brilliantly as he writes, "Like newborn babies, crave pure spiritual milk, so that by it you may grow up in your salvation." The believer who has been initiated into spiritual growth ought to be stimulated to growth on an ongoing basis. The baby with no appetite is a sick baby. Believers without appetites for spiritual growth are deficient in spiritual experience. A desire for growth needs to be stimulated.

Now you'll notice in your Bible, if you are using the *New International Version* as I am, it says that we are to "crave pure spiritual milk." Some of you may be using the *King James Version* in which you'll find the familiar expression, "As newborn babies, desire the sincere milk of the word." More modern translations, like the *NIV*, have made changes. The Greek word for "word" is *logos*. Greeks, when they thought in terms of "word" (*logos*), also thought in terms of reason behind the words. The reasonable, rational part of the human being was, in their thinking, the spiritual part. So when they used the word *logos* it could mean "word," "reason," "rationality" or "spirituality." All these things were wrapped up in the word. The word Peter uses here which is translated "spiritual" in the *NIV* and "of the word" in the *KJV* is *logikos*. Accordingly, in some places "the milk" is the Word of God, but in other places it means "all that is spiritual." We will use this broader understanding of the "spiritual milk" we are to crave to point out five things that will stimulate valid spiritual growth.

First, the stimulation by hearing the Word of God. If we understand that spiritual experience is initiated through the proclamation of the Word of God we should find no difficulty understanding that spiritual growth is also related to the Word of God. There are three major ways in which an appetite can be stimulated through the Word of God. First, the place of attending to the preaching of the Word on a regular, thoughtful, prayerful basis.

Second, the personal daily devotional habit of feasting on the Word and, thirdly, the participation with others in small groups or one-on-one situations where there can be a sharing of the Word. All these opportunities for growth should be warmly embraced.

Second, the stimulation created by knowing the Son of God. Three ingredients are necessary if we are to know people. First, we need to talk to them. By talking I mean having dialogue—listening to them so that we know what they are saying and feeling. Talking to them so that they know how we're responding to what they are saying. Second, we need to spend some time with them. It needs to be what we call somewhat euphemistically, "quality time," which, from my experience, requires accessibility—they have to be able to get to us, and availability—they have to feel they've got us when they got *to* us. Third, we need to trust people. It is only by trusting that we find out what people are made of. Dependability is demonstrated only by giving people the chance to let you down. Getting to know somebody better takes talk, time and trust.

Growth in knowledge of the Lord Jesus is very similar. We must build into our lives the opportunity to talk with Him. Life situations where we have to trust Him must be welcomed rather than dreaded and avoided. Take time to be with Him in the quiet place but also learn to practice His presence in the busy places. When we are tempted to say there are not enough hours in a day, we must remember God has given the exact right number of hours to do what is necessary.

Third, the stimulation created by experiences of the life of God. It is all too easy to lower the sights of our Christian attainment so that we feel satisfied with our spiritual achievements. If we aim low enough there is not the same fear of failure. This can lead to misplaced contentment and disinterest in spiritual growth. Let me give you an example. The Bible does not say "Rejoice in the Lord sometimes." What it actually says is, "Rejoice in the Lord always" (Phil. 4:4). The "always" requires a high aim—the "sometimes" is much more manageable. When I wake up on a nice morning I feel good, so I rejoice and I attribute it to the Lord and say, "Good morning, Lord." I rejoice in the Lord. But when I wake up to 18 inches of snow, 15 degrees below zero, my car won't start, my boss chews me out and I can't watch Monday night football because I've got a meeting, rejoicing is not an option if I operate on the "sometime" basis.

Suppose I decide to think, "The Bible says what it means and means what it says; therefore, it means rejoice in the Lord always and that's going to take more than I've got!" As soon as I come to that conclusion I start being interested in more than my ability. The indwelling presence of the living Lord Jesus becomes a vital concern. If we lower our sights to the level of our attainment, all it takes to live it is ourselves. But if we raise our sights according to Scripture, all it takes to live it is ourselves related to Him. We create a desire for spiritual growth in terms of the life of God when we desire to live in accordance with God's Word, not according to carefully revised and selected portions.

Fourth, the stimulation created by relating to the people of God. It is possible to live our lives spiritually, alone. We do our own thing, we go our own way, we don't interfere with anybody, we don't let anybody interfere with us. But this doesn't promote much growth. The family is the place for growth. There we really know who people are because they speak freely, react instinctively, relate honestly and live supportively. It is in that kind of an environment that we come to terms with ourselves, examine our exposed frailties and take steps to live harmoniously even with those with whom we find tension. The spiritual family is not just people in pews on Sunday sitting in a large crowd, retaining their anonymity. The true spiritual family is a group of believers where there is mutual commitment and healthy interaction. In such an environment it is easy to identify prejudices and presuppositions, weaknesses and strengths, gifts and lack of them. We level with each other and confront each other, correct each other and reprove, rebuke and encourage each other; therein lies growth.

The Consolidation of Spiritual Growth

Is it possible to measure spiritual growth? Can we know if we are growing up spiritually? Peter seemed to think so and he particularly addresses the subject of relationships. He says in verse 1, "Therefore, rid yourselves of all malice and all deceit, hypocrisy, envy, and slander of every kind." There is a definite link between tasting that the Lord is good, hearing the Word, being born again of the Spirit, craving spiritual milk and growing. In this context Peter shows that growth is clearly measurable in relationships. This requires particular attention to identifying things that are wrong and dealing with them.

Recognition of our behavior. I have learned in

my interpersonal relationships that very few other people perceive me to be what I perceive myself to be. In the same way my perceptions of others are often far removed from their self-perceptions.

We can recognize our behavior through the Word of God. Peter learned this the hard way. One day when Jesus told His disciples about His impending death and resurrection, Peter interposed his considerable bulk between the Lord Jesus and Jerusalem and said, "Not so, Lord." The response of the Lord Jesus practically blew Peter out of the water, "Get thee behind me, Satan" (Matt. 16:23). Peter was doing what he thought was right. Everybody else was thinking the same thing but Peter wasn't just thinking it, he was speaking out! But he could not perceive what was behind his own behavior until Jesus, almost brutally, showed him the reality of his action. If we would carefully and assiduously put our behavior under the spotlight of the Word of God we would have similar shocks to the one Peter experienced.

We can recognize our behavior through the example of the Lord Jesus. Peter went fishing with the Lord Jesus on one occasion. He was a good fisherman who knew exactly what he was doing, but he caught nothing. Jesus suggested a different approach which Peter agreed to, and to his amazement the net came out so full of fish that it began to break. Peter fell down in front of the Lord Jesus and said, "Go away from me, Lord; I am a sinful man" (Luke 5:8). This remarkable reaction was not triggered by a net full of fish but by the realization of who the Lord Jesus really is. A good way to evaluate behavior, after you put it under the searchlight of the Word of God, is to put it alongside the example of Jesus Christ.

We can recognize our behavior by confrontation with believers. Peter was no stranger to confrontation. He was involved in the controversy about Gentile believers' responsibility to the Jewish religion. Unfortunately, he had said one thing and then he had done another, and his inconsistency had compounded the problem. When Paul arrived on the scene he read the situation and promptly set up a meeting with Peter and "opposed him to his face" (Gal. 2:11). Confrontation among believers can be destructive or creative. Done in the wrong spirit it can decimate a brother, but when done properly it can bring forth positive results. I learned in the early days of my ministry that to confront people we must earn the right to do it by proving our love for those people.

Repentance for behavior. Psychologists and psychiatrists have greatly helped modern man to understand modern man. We know a lot more about human behavior than ever before, but unfortunately, some of the understandings are misunderstandings. A specialist in human behavior can identify the factors that lead to an action, but if he then assumes that the factors alone are to blame and the person is not responsible, he will arrive at a dangerous conclusion. He will see all actions as the result of circumstances rather than choice and, accordingly, prescribe therapy rather than repentance. In many instances therapy must include repentance for sin in the same way that repentant sinners often need therapy to deal with the factors that led to the sin.

Rejection of behavior. First there is the rejection of *malice*. The Bible uses different Greek words to describe anger. There is "short fuse" anger which is volcanic in nature and expressive.

Then there is "slow burn" anger which is a cold, hard, settled resentment devoted to getting even. That's malice, and it must be rejected, thrown away like dirty clothes. How is it done? By a commitment to help the one who harmed rather than adding more harm to the harm done.

Second is the rejection of *guile*. Guile is a desire to deceive or to mislead. Sometimes we do it because honesty is too painful. Rather than telling the truth in love which might help to heal we often take a line that is perilously close to "lying lovingly"! Guile can be lying in Sunday clothes, but these clothes too need to be ripped off.

Third, the rejection of *hypocrisy*. Hypocrisy is playacting—being one thing inside and another thing outside. Why do we do it? Because we want people to think highly of us and we fear the truth may be so unpleasant that we will lose their love and respect. But this attitude is not conducive to growth. It must be rejected. Instead of having an inordinate tendency to conceal, we must recognize the necessity to confess.

Fourth, the rejection of *envy*. What is envy? Envy is resentment that another person is or has something you neither are nor have. Peter was possibly threatened by John because he was young and smart and special to Christ. When he was told how he would die he immediately asked, pointing to John, "What about him?" The Lord gave him some very helpful advice, telling him in effect, "Peter, you have only got two things to do. Number one, mind your own business and number two, follow me!" (see John 21:21,22). That's the best advice on how to handle envy!

Fifth, the rejection of *slander*. Slander is speaking against somebody, and it is such fun, but it is illegitimate fun and must be discarded. Some simple rules help in this difficult assignment. Before speaking against somebody ask yourself, "Is it true—really true—do I know it's true?" Secondly, "Is it fair—is it part truth—is it selectively indifferent to some pieces of data?" Thirdly, "Is it necessary—what will the sharing of this information achieve that is constructive?" One of the best ways of helping other people to reject slander is to stop listening to them!

Spiritual growth is evidence of life and health in the Spirit. Having been initiated it must be stimulated to be consolidated. Interpersonal relationships are a clear measure of maturity and require much effort in the power of the Spirit.

EIGHT

BUILDING ON THE ROCK
1 Peter 2:4-8

Long before he was Peter, the Galilean fisherman was called Simeon. The Greek equivalent by which he was also known was Simon and, in addition, his Aramaic name was Cephas. The Lord Jesus decided he didn't have enough names so He called him *Petros* or "Peter." *Petros* is the masculine form of *Petra*—a "rock." It's interesting that rocks are feminine in Greek! So it would be perfectly legitimate to call this man by his formal names—Simeon, Simon, Cephas, or by the nickname Christ gave him—"Rocky."

If we think of Peter as Rocky we will remember that the Lord made a very powerful statement concerning Peter being the rock. When He said, "You are Peter [Rocky], and on this rock I will build my church" (Matt. 16:18), He said something that has given theologians grounds for debate ever since. Roman Catholic theologians, of course, have pointed out with some considerable justification that the Lord Jesus was saying that Peter was the rock on which the church was going to be built. The Reformers, who had a hard time with some aspects of Catholic theology, objected to this idea and its resultant traditions and insisted "the rock" was not Peter but the confession that Peter made that Jesus was the Christ. We don't need to get into this discussion because whatever Peter's role as the leader of the apostles, who were called the foundation of the church, we do know that Peter pointed to Jesus and called Him "the living stone." There is therefore no question that, whatever human agencies are involved in the church, it is Christ Himself who is the Rock, the Living Stone. Not only that, the Apostle Peter says that all believers are "living stones" built upon the Living Stone—Christ—in order that they might become an edifice in which God dwells by His Spirit.

When the going gets tough it's very important that we have a solid foundation under our feet. The Lord told about the man who built a beautiful house on the sand but when the wind came the house fell down. Then, in contrast, He told about the man who built his house on the rock—the same kind of house, wind, and waves, but this house stood firm. When the going gets tough many people collapse because they have built a magnificent edifice on sand. It is important that we check how we're building, what we're building and where we're building. Peter tells us that we need to build on the Rock, and that Rock is Christ.

Christ—The Living Stone

When we talk about Christ the Living Stone, we are thinking of Christ in a particular capacity. In order to understand this there are three things we need to look at.

First, in the Old Testament there is a prophetic pronouncement concerning the Living Stone. The prophet Isaiah wrote: "The Lord Almighty is the one you are to regard as holy, he is the one you are to fear, he is the one you are to dread, and he will be a sanctuary; but for both houses of Israel he will be a stone that causes men to stumble and a rock that makes them fall" (Isa. 8:13,14). He was telling them what they ought to fear and what they ought not to fear. He told those who were worried about a political conspiracy, the economic conditions, and societal problems not to worry about such things, but rather to fear the Lord, because their problems were fundamentally spiritual rather than political or societal. Those who fear Him will find Him to be a sanctuary; but those who disregard Him in their obsession with more mundane matters will stumble and fall when they face His judgment. He, to them, will be a stumbling stone.

The prophet later returned to his theme saying: "See, I lay a stone in Zion, a tested stone, a precious cornerstone for a sure foundation; the one who trusts will never be dismayed" (Isa. 28:16). Isaiah's contemporaries were all confused, taking refuge in untruth, living in a fantasy world, disregarding absolute standards, living in a maze of relativity. But in the midst of the confusion, God has put a Rock that is absolutely true and stable. This Rock will become the standard of righteousness and the basis of justice.

When we turn to Psalm 118, which was sung by the pilgrims climbing the steep ascent to the Temple in Jerusalem, we read: "The stone the builders rejected has become the capstone; the Lord has done this, and it is marvelous in our eyes. This is the day the Lord has made; let us rejoice and be glad in it" (Ps. 118:22-24). We are not certain when this psalm of jubilation was written so we cannot identify with certainty the rejected stone which became the Cornerstone! Some use this as a reference to the fact that the Temple, which was David's idea, was built even though God rejected David's request to build it. Others see it as a reference to the Temple being rebuilt after it had been destroyed as the people of God were humiliated by their enemies. Either way the theme is the same— jubilation because God restored what He had judged. The rock in the Old Testament is therefore a symbol of judgment, justice and jubilation.

Second, on turning to the New Testament we find in Mark 12 a messianic parable. The Lord told a story of a man who planted a vineyard, put a wall around it, dug a pit for the winepress, built a watchtower, rented the vineyard to some farmers and went away on a journey. At harvest time he sent servants to collect the rent and the fruit, but the farmers seized them, beat them up and sent them away empty-handed. Finally the owner sent his son, believing his tenants would respect him; but they beat him up too. Having told this parable the Lord linked it with the stone the builders rejected which became the capstone, and then showed that He was the Old Testament Stone and the New Testament Son. He was laying claim to being the basis of judgment and justice and jubilation. He was the One of whom the prophets spoke, none other than the Son rejected by the tenants but accepted by the Father and promised to be the chief Cornerstone. (See Mark 12:1-11.)

Then, third, we need to look for the apostolic teaching. In Acts 4 we find Peter preaching before the Sanhedrin. He is in trouble because he healed someone, and the authorities are asking, "By what power or what name did you [heal this man]?" His answer is straightforward, "By the name of Jesus Christ of Nazareth, whom you crucified but whom God raised from the dead,. . . this man stands before you completely healed. He is 'the stone you builders rejected, which has become the capstone' " (Acts 4:7-11). If we weren't sure of the prophetic pronouncement and if we had a problem with the messianic parable we shouldn't have any difficulty with the apostolic teaching! The rejected stone, Peter says, is the crucified Christ. The capstone is Christ exalted.

Let me explain about the capstone. The builders of Solomon's Temple were given instructions that no sound of tools was to be heard at the Temple site, so all the stones were cut out of the quarry, dressed, shaped and transported and immediately put into place. These immense stones had to be cut exactly right, and without plaster or cement they had to fit together. The secret was the capstone—the final unit which was intricately cut, beveled and angled—uniquely fitted for its crucial role of holding the whole edifice together. Like a jigsaw puzzle holds together when the last piece fits—so the capstone brought everything together, and only the stone specially prepared would fit. This stone, Peter told the Sanhedrin, is Jesus—rejected, crucified, risen and exalted.

Christ is also the "cornerstone," the foundation of the main corner upon which everything is built. Jesus Christ is the One upon whom God has built everything. Peter puts it this way: "Salvation is found in no one else, for there is no other name under heaven given to men by which we must be saved" (Acts 4:12). In our contemporary world there are attempts to take the best of Christianity, Buddhism, Islam, Shintoism and other religions, bring them together and make out of them a universal religion where everybody can be together and everybody can believe the same thing. The problem for Christians is that the apostles taught that Christ and Christ alone is the rock upon which God is building everything, that Christ and Christ alone is the capstone that will make everything fit together, and there is salvation in no other.

When we approach Christ as the Living Stone we need to draw from Peter's rich knowledge of the Old Testament. The children of Israel traveling through the wilderness were thirsty and disgruntled. God told Moses to go to a rock, smite it with his rod and out of the rock waters would flow. It became a living stone—a living rock. There was a tradition among the Hebrews that this rock followed them in the wilderness, and you'll find Paul using this idea in 1 Corinthians 10, where he says this living rock is Christ. Now we see another picture of Christ as the Living Stone from whom life originates. Spiritual life and nourishment are to be found in Him and in Him alone.

As we stated in a previous chapter, during the Feast of Tabernacles the people went to Jerusalem to commemorate the time when their forefathers were in the wilderness and Moses smote the rock from which the water flowed. The chief priest standing before the assembled congregation poured water, that had been collected from the spring, out of a pitcher. On one occasion Christ shouted from the crowd, "If a man is thirsty, let him come to me and drink. Whoever believes in me ... streams of living water will flow from within

him" (John 7:37,38). He was insisting that He was
the reality behind the ritual—the Rock from whom
the living waters come.

Peter points out, however, that this stone can
also be a stumbling stone to some people. Those
who reject Christ, whom God has chosen and who
is not going to move or change, will stumble over
Him and will fall into a spiritual lostness. That, in
essence, is the divine revelation of the living
stone—the prophetic, the messianic and the apostolic revelation.

Now let's look at the human reaction to all this.
We talk a lot about human freedom and human
rights, and we must remember that we have them
because they were God-ordained. One of the greatest is the freedom to react to what God has
revealed. Peter says that some people "stumble
because they disobey the message—which is also
what they were destined for" (1 Pet. 2:8). It's interesting to notice that the Greek word translated
"destined" is the same one that is translated "lay."
In the same way that the builder lays the foundation stone and it is settled in the place of his
choice, so God has "settled" the consequences of
man's choices. Man is free to react as he wishes to
the message of Christ, the Living Stone; but God
has the absolute right to determine the consequences of man's choice. God has reserved for
man the freedom to choose and has reserved for
Himself the freedom to determine the consequences of that choice; and He has laid it like a
rock—there it stands! Nothing will change it.

God has ordained that those who respond to
the message of the Living Stone will find that, as
they build their lives on Him, they will never be put
to shame. There is utter security in Him. On the

other hand, God says that those who choose to reject Him will find a stone of stumbling instead of a stone of security. They'll stub toes on Him every day. They'll bump up against His truth constantly. They'll trip over the convicting work of the Holy Spirit and stumble over the barriers that God is putting in their pathway to hell. But they'll go on tripping, stumbling and falling until in the end they will fall, still rejecting Him, into a lost eternity.

Christians—The Living Stones

Having developed one application of the Living Stone, Peter goes on to develop another. He writes, "You also, like living stones, are being built into a spiritual house to be a holy priesthood, offering spiritual sacrifices acceptable to God through Jesus Christ" (2:5). This means, first of all, that the Lord Jesus wants to have a very special relationship with those who choose to be related to Him. In the same way that He is called the Living Stone He wants us to be called living stones too. It reminds me of what He said about being "the light of the world." "So long as I am in the world," He said, "I am the light of the world." But then He added to His disciples, "When I'm no longer here you are the light of the world." (See John 8:12; 9:15; Matt. 5:14.) In short, when we become believers we are called to perpetuate that which Christ started, to project that which Christ is. He is the Light but we become the lights of the world. He is the Living Stone but after He is gone we become the living stones. So we establish a very definite and simple relationship with Him. The A.B.C.D. of this relationship is as follows:

A. *We admit*—we admit the truth concerning

Him and ourselves; truth that we may have chosen to avoid; truths that we may have resisted; the truth of our spiritual condition and His saving merit.

B. *We believe*—we trust that what God says about ourselves is right—we trust that what God says about His Son is right. We come deeply to believe these things to such an extent that we stake everything on Him.

C. *We come* to Him. The one way that we can come is repentantly and submissively. We come to Him and say, "Lord Jesus, I am the sinner you died to save. I'm the rebel over whom you wish to reign. I am living out here in a cold, chaotic stone yard and I need to be built into who you are and to what you're doing. I come to you and I surrender myself to you."

D. *We discover*—the reality of all the things of which we have been speaking. This can be summarized in the words of verse 7, "Now to you who believe, this stone is precious." Only those who believe find Christ infinitely precious. Only those who come to Him find Him infinitely rich. Only those to whom the Spirit of God is speaking find this truth overwhelmingly beautiful. We can always know if we've become a living stone built upon the Living Stone by determining if Jesus Christ is precious to us. Living stones start to live like the Living Stone. He is not only Saviour and Lord but our model too. We aspire to be like Him.

The apostle moreover points out that living stones "are being built into a spiritual house" (v. 5). This is a picture of the stones being cut in the quarry and built into a temple. The New Testament tells us quite clearly that individual believers are cut out of the quarry of society and transported into a place where their lives are fit together with other lives, and they are built into the church of Jesus Christ to be the temple of the Holy Spirit. God is alive in our midst and doing something to His glory and man's blessing. Peter was never one to worry about mixed metaphors! He said that we're not only the temple but we're the priests serving in the temple. We have become a holy priesthood. That means that every believer has a gift with which to develop a ministry.

Not only that, we engage in a life of "spiritual sacrifice." A life of ministry is a life of sacrifice, a life of service. Lives built on sand crumble; lives built on the Rock triumph. Jesus Christ is either utter security or the basis of stumbling. Identified with Him we become living stones, built up in a fellowship of believers, exercising a spiritual priesthood, engaging in a ministry, and living a life of sacrifice. In tough times we don't need sandstone, we need Christ—Rock. And we need never wonder if we are built on Him because the evidence is clear. When we are sure of our foundation, we have little to fear and tough times are nowhere near as tough.

NINE

GOD'S SUPPORT GROUP
1 Peter 2:9-12

If there is one thing worse than loneliness it is facing tough times alone. God never intended this for believers. They face tough times not on their own, but in the special community of the redeemed. Peter is careful to emphasize "the people" aspect of spiritual experience in his Epistle. He uses three different Greek words in these verses to give the idea of a *people*, a *race* and a *nation*. His objective is to remind the believers of the strength and security to be found in shared experience. It is a rare privilege to belong to God's people and share in their blessings.

He uses a rich variety of words to describe this privilege. He says we are a chosen people, a royal priesthood, a holy nation, a people belonging to God." Every privileged position brings its own peculiar pressures but those who enjoy the blessings and appreciate the advantages of the corporate nature of spiritual experiences do not shirk the pressures.

The Place of Privilege

Once more we find Peter drawing his ideas from the Old Testament. The expressions "chosen people, royal priesthood, holy nation and people belonging to God" are not original to Peter; they came from his study of Exodus 19 and Isaiah 43. But he does not hesitate to apply the ancient concepts of the people of God to the Christian believers scattered throughout the Roman provinces, and, of course, we recognize that we follow in their train. There are two things we should notice about the place of privilege—the privilege of becoming a people and the privilege of being a priesthood.

There are a number of words to describe the privilege of becoming a people. First of all he calls us *"a chosen people"!* Peter has already told the people that they have been chosen according to the foreknowledge of God. God has always freely chosen to call "a people" to Himself. He chose to make of Abraham a great people. He narrowed it down to Isaac, not Ishmael, and further determined to work through Jacob rather than Esau. The progeny of Jacob became known as the people of Israel. You remember that He set His hand upon them, brought them out of Egypt, and placed them in the land of promise. Then He said that there they would function as a nation, as a people, as a race distinct from the other nations. His objective was that they might clearly demonstrate to other nations what a nation is like when God is its Lord. They were a chosen people. There is a sense in which God chooses individuals to be certain things; but we need to bear in mind that God has chosen to work through "peoples" and communities, and individuals must see themselves as part of these bodies.

The Preamble to the Constitution states, "We the people of the United States, in order to form a more perfect Union, establish Justice, ensure domestic Tranquility, provide for the common defence, promote the general Welfare, and secure the Blessings of Liberty to ourselves and our Posterity, do ordain and establish this Constitution of the United States of America." Notice that it is not a group of individuals saying, "Okay, gang, we're going to do our own thing. Let it all hang out. If it feels good it must be right. Have fun!" This kind of thinking is a more recent development. If the United States had started off on that basis, frankly there would be no nation. There would not be "a people"; but because there was a decision by a number of individuals to submerge their individuality for the common good, a nation was born.

God doesn't just call individuals to Himself to save them and let them do their own thing. He calls them to be a people whose objective will be to produce a more perfect union, to work towards the establishing of justice and righteousness and interpersonal relationships. When they sense that people in the fellowship are not enjoying domestic tranquility they commit themselves to assist in attaining it. If they recognize that some people are under attack, they commit themselves to the common defense; and if some are impoverished and some are in need and others have an abundance, they commit themselves to the general welfare of the fellowship of believers. This is the state of high privilege God has chosen for us. The church is not an exclusive club; it is a group of the committed— committed to Christ and His people, and God has chosen it should be this way.

Secondly, we are called *"a holy people."* We are

already familiar with the word *holy* but we may remind ourselves that in this context it means that the people of God are a separate people—they have a distinctive identity. This is seen in Christian behavior quite clearly. For instance, when God's people meet, meet with them. They don't do the things the rest of the world is doing. They say, "I have a commitment to this group, and if they worship, I worship with them. When they give, I give." But the word *holy* also has the connotation of purity. Some of the things common to our world just don't belong in the people of God. When we identify with the people of God there is a distinctive rejection of much which unbelievers condone and embrace. To engage in such things brings discredit to the people with whom we identify and harm to the name of the One to whom we owe allegiance.

Thirdly, we are called *"a special people."* Peter says we are "a people belonging to God." That translation doesn't do justice to the word Peter used. When I was a small boy I learned a hymn that contained the words, "When He cometh, when He cometh to make up His jewels." I learned it so well I can't remember any more! I remember thinking about that hymn and saying to my mother, "Mother, who are Jesus' jewels?" And she said, "You are." So I strutted around like a little jewel for a while. Then I forgot all about it. Years later I was reading Malachi 3:17, "They will be mine . . . When I make up my jewels," and I realized that the hymn writer got his idea from Malachi. But so did Peter, for the word he uses is exactly the same as was used in the Greek translation of Malachi 3:17. The expression which says that we are a people belonging to God means, literally, that we are purchased at tremendous cost and therefore are as precious as a jewel to His heart. We are a special people to God. That's a privilege.

Fourthly, we are *"a called people."* We are intended to "declare the praises of him who called [us] out of darkness into his wonderful light." The "call" in Scripture means "to give a name." We use the word *call* this way. I am called Stuart Briscoe because I was born of the Briscoes and they chose to give me the first name Stuart. But the word *call* also means "to invite somebody into an experience, a status, or a position." So the call of God to individuals is that they might be invited from the position in which they find themselves into a new situation where they will have a new name—His name. It is rather like being called out of darkness into His most marvelous light. The initiative or the call starts with God. It is He who calls, invites and who invades our darkness. Charles Wesley said it wonderfully:
"Long my imprisoned spirit lay,
fast bound in sin and nature's night,
Thine eye diffused a quickening ray,
I woke, the dungeon flamed with light,
My chains fell off,
My heart was free, I rose, went forth
and followed thee."

But God doesn't do it just for individuals, He does it for a people called together into this light.

Fifthly, we are *"a pitied people"* too. Peter writes: "Once you were not a people, but now you are the people of God; once you had not received mercy, but now you have received mercy," and this time he quotes Hosea (2:23).

You may wonder why I chose the word *pitied*. It

is the real meaning of the word translated "mercy."
As Jesus and His disciples were coming out of
Jericho they met a blind man called Bartimaeus.
When he realized Jesus was there he called out at
the top of his voice, "Jesus, thou Son of David,
make sure that I receive my constitutional rights."
No, he didn't! He said, "Jesus, Son of David, have
mercy on me!" (See Mark 10:46-52.) I'm all in favor
of human rights, particularly if we bear in mind
from Whom we derive whatever rights we have.
But if we forget Him we may get the idea that we
deserve something and therefore we can demand
everything; when in actual fact if we bear in mind
the One from whom we claim our rights, we know
we deserve only His condemnation and therefore
prefer to plead for mercy rather than demand our
rights. Once we were not a people but now we are
because, when we asked Him to give us what we
have never earned, He pitied us and made us His
people. The lovely thing about the people of God is
that they have no pretensions because they know
their only claim to fame is that they asked for
mercy and graciously it was granted to them!

*Peter also talks about the privilege of being a
"priesthood."* The expression "royal priesthood"
suggests that believers come together as a *community of kings*, and when they come together they
are also a *priesthood*. Let's take the second one
first.

For many years the church seemed to think
there were two kinds of Christians, the clergy and
the laity. Incidentally, one of the Greek words that
is translated "people" in this passage is the word
from which we get the word *laity*. The clergy were
perceived to have a very special "in" with God.
They acted as intermediaries, and without them

the common folks couldn't really get to Him. There was a great emphasis on this for centuries, and in some segments of the church the concept persists. Sometimes church architecture keeps the clergy separate from the laity so they have to peer over feathered hats into the dim distance to where the clergy are doing the religion for the people. This is all very unfortunate because the Bible actually teaches that the church is a fellowship comprised of priests, all of whom have a ministry, exercise gifts and offer spiritual sacrifices to Him, and all are involved in building up the Body of Christ.

We also are a kingdom, which means that we are called together, as Paul wrote, "[to] reign in life through the one man, Jesus Christ" (Rom. 5:17). The writer of Proverbs said, "A king is stately in his progress"; and the expression, *a kingdom* suggests a group of kings—people who are called to stride through life with a degree of regal bearing, not stumbling, not staggering, but striding over what other people sink under. We can't do it individually, but as a community of kings and a community of priests we are a privileged people and this greatly raises the possibilities of our living in tough times.

The Price of Privilege
Peter, when he called believers "aliens and strangers in the world" (1 Pet. 2:11), was reminding us that we must *accept our status*. He has already mentioned this idea in the first chapter.

In January of every year all resident aliens in the United States of America have to fill out forms to show where they are living and to prove that they are still being good. Before I took American citizenship I used to complete five forms for my family. But now, as the other four retained their former citizenship, I supply the forms and tell them, "If you want to stay in my country, fill out the forms and we'll see what we can do for you!"

There is a difference between being a citizen and an alien. Now this is what Peter says: "If you are a member of the people of God, you are, to a certain extent, an alien and a stranger to the rest of society." Part of the price that believers pay for the privilege of being "a people" is that they are aliens among the citizens of this world and, although they may resent it, they must accept this status. This requires a declaration of difference.

When I first came over to the United States I used to speak at luncheons where the people would stand, face the flag, and put their hands on their hearts. At first I thought they had angina. Then they would pledge allegiance to the flag. I was always embarrassed because I couldn't join them as it wasn't my flag, but I was stuck up on the platform with everybody looking at me assuming I was a Communist. I had to try to explain to them that I was making a declaration of difference. This declaration also necessitates a degree of detachment.

When I was just a kid of 18 I played on a rugby team for the Royal Marines. The rugby was great, but the time after the game was dreadful. The bus stopped at every pub on the way home and my teammates slowly drank themselves into oblivion while I waited alone on the bus. But I stayed with them, made a declaration of difference, developed a degree of detachment, and put most of them to bed! It was all part of the price of privilege!

The second part of the price is that we *abstain from seductions*. Peter wrote, "Dear friends, I urge you . . . to abstain from sinful desires, which war against your soul" (v. 11). All of us are subject to temptations and seductions outside us to which we readily respond through the sinful desires within us. If we drop our guard we will be vulnerable to things which "war against the soul"! Some of you have been in wars, you have smelled war, you have walked through the ravages of war. You have seen brave men die and innocent people suffer in wars, and you'll never forget it. War is a beastly business.

When we give way to sinful desires, whether it be the abuse of sex or of appetite, anger or bitterness, jealousy, envy or any kind of hostility, war enters our souls. These things do as much damage to our souls as a tank driving through a plot of violets. Our lives, instead of being like the sweet countryside where the quiet rivers flow through meadows and slumbering villages, become like a battlefield littered with great craters full of muddy water, mechanical wreckage, and the carnage of destroyed bodies. I'm not overdoing it because Peter uses a powerful word here.

Do you sometimes wonder why God seems so distant, why prayer is such a bore, why worship is of no interest, why fellowship with God's people is something you don't desire? Do you wonder why the sweet things of the Spirit sometimes feel totally foreign to you? It's because somewhere, somehow, under some circumstances you succumbed to sinful desires within you because of the seductive influences outside you. They warred against your soul, and instead of the sweetness and the beauty of a spiritual life there is the barrenness and the bleakness of a battlefield. The price of privilege is to abstain in the power of the Spirit of God from those things which war against the soul. We probably can't do it on our own, but that's why God made us members of a "people" who will support us in the struggle.

The price of privilege also means we must *absorb the slander*. The apostle wrote, "Though they accuse you of doing wrong, they may see your good deeds and glorify God on the day he visits [you]" (v. 12). The early Christians were subjected to all kinds of abuse and slander. Athenagorus, a Christian philosopher from Athens, wrote "A Plea for Christians" in AD 177 and addressed it to Marcus Aurelius and Lucius Aurelius, the Roman emperors. What he said in effect was that the Christians were getting a raw deal; they were accused of all kinds of things and everybody was believing the accusations. The specific charges were that they were engaging in the practice of "Atheism, Thyestian Feasts and Oedipodean Intercourse."

Can you imagine the Christians being accused of atheism by pagans? The pagans worshiped a multiplicity of gods and the Christians refused to join them. Anybody who refused to worship the gods of the nation and national security and national prosperity, in pagan thinking, must be an atheist. In actual fact Christians had discovered the true God and rejected the false gods, but they had to endure the ignominy of being accused by pagans of being what the pagans were themselves.

Then they were accused of attending Thyestian feasts. Thyestes was a man who organized banquets where the delicacy was human flesh. In other words a Thyestian feast was a cannibalistic feast. The pagans accused the Christians of cannibalism. They had heard them quote the Lord

Jesus, "Except you eat my body and drink my blood you have no life in you." They had heard that He said, "This is my body. This is my blood," and told them to eat and drink. The pagans said, "You know what they do? They turn bread into flesh and wine into blood. They are cannibals." There was utter revulsion against the Christians!

Not only that, they were accused of Oedipodean intercourse. We all know about Oedipus who was adopted as a child, grew up, saw a delightful lady, married her and found out eventually that he had married his mother. Freud gave them both a lot of publicity as he propagated his theories of sexual development, with particular reference to incestuous tendencies. But long before Freud, people were having trouble in this area, and the pagans were accusing the Christians of incestuous behavior. You see the Christians called all the women "sisters." The men of the church had very close relationships with these "sisters" so the pagans, in their ignorance, put two and two together and came up with six. Not long ago in the church we kept the women with the women and the men with the men to avoid any appearance of impropriety. But now, of course, if women are seen with women our critics assume they are lesbians and men with men are homosexuals! When a Christian tries to live in an unchristian society he can be certain that just about everything he stands for will be rejected, and much that he does will be misinterpreted, and he may well be slandered from beginning to end. So you know what he has to do? Absorb it! And how does he do that? By standing firm in his own conviction about the truth and waiting for the final judgment when God will reveal the secrets of men's hearts. And that's all part of the price of privilege.

The Practice of Privilege

Privileged people recognize that privilege brings opportunity as well as responsibility. We have the opportunity to "declare the praises of him who called [us] out of darkness into his wonderful light" (v. 9). We must therefore *declare the virtues of the God who is above us*. To be silent in the place of blessing is to fail in the seat of privilege. To say nothing of the virtues of God in the environment of His grace is to border on the insulting. It takes a conscious effort not to declare that in which we delight; but to speak is as natural as to enjoy.

Secondly, we need to *decline the vices of the society around us*. In verse 12 Peter says, "Live such good lives among the pagans . . ." Among the pagans—that's where we live. We dare not, we must not isolate ourselves. There is a great tendency for believers to pull out from society and to protect themselves from every outside influence. When it goes to the extreme of Christian isolation from pagans it is unbiblical and dangerous. It's dangerous for the Christian and disastrous for the pagan. Where do we live? We live among the pagans. How do we live? We live unlike the pagans. We live "good lives" among the pagans.

Thirdly, we begin to *define the values of the world against us*. Peter may be thinking back to the Sermon on the Mount when the Lord told His disciples that they were "salt" and "light" and that they were to let their "good works" be seen so that the observers might "glorify God." In other words, the pagans are going to see the good deeds and recognize their goodness; but how are pagans going to recognize they are good if they have a different standard of values? Only when Christians begin to turn *them* around instead of being turned around. We have to define values for the world. If they don't see Christian goodness they will have no knowledge or experience of it.

There is a place for believers in the midst of a pagan society—a challenging position of change and conflict fraught with problems and full of difficulties. For the fainthearted this is threatening; for the noble-minded, exciting.

TEN

THE CHRISTIAN CITIZEN
1 Peter 2:12-17

As Christians we are citizens of heaven, and our permanent residence is there, but we live temporarily on earth. The way we live down here as citizens, recognizing the political and economic and sociological structures of the society in which we live, is very important. We're not just spiritual people living in a spiritual vacuum; our true spirituality is demonstrated as we live in the midst of a secular society.

There are three particular areas of concern that Peter mentions which relate to our unique position in secular society—authority, liberty and dignity.

Authority and the Christian Citizen
Now Christians, of all people, *understand and recognize the place of authority*. They understand authority in principle because they believe in God—the Supreme Being from whom we come, through whom we survive and to whom we go.

They believe we are answerable to Him because the very concept of God means that in Him ultimate authority resides. It is impossible to believe that God exists and not to believe in authority as a principle.

Christians also believe that our world was created and that it operates on discernible laws and principles. If this were not the case science would be a nonsense. But science assumes that there are discernible and predictable laws, and it is not surprising that early scientific endeavors were motivated by Christians who believed in laws, principles and authority.

Christians also believe that human beings are sinful and, because of this, authority is necessary in order that society might be made tolerable. C.S. Lewis said he was in favor of democracy, not because everybody is equally intelligent or equally qualified to have an equal say, but because everybody is equally sinful and we all need to keep an eye on each other! Christians recognize that all equally sinful people need principles of authority to keep us in check. Christian belief presupposes belief in authority.

Christians also have good insights into the practice of authority. They recognize, as Peter says in verse 13, that authority has been instituted "for the Lord's sake" and it is to be submitted to because "it is God's will" (v. 14). Paul, in Romans 13, develops this theme much more fully, explaining that authority is ordained of God. According to him there is no authority except that which God has established. Consequently, he who rebels against authority is rebelling against what God has instituted and will bring judgment on himself. We live in an antinomian age where people reject and resent authority. People are more concerned with individual freedoms and liberties than with being responsible members of society acknowledging the authorities. It is particularly important, therefore, that Christians maintain their special understanding of authority and show it in life-style and behavior.

Not only that, Christians recognize what the authorities are supposed to do. Paul summarizes it very succinctly. He says that the authority is ordained to punish those who do wrong and to reward those who do right. One of the ways that Christian citizens live distinctively is by having a high view of authority and responding properly to it.

Now let us consider the Christian's response to authority. The Christian response to authority is one of submission. There are three reasons for this. First of all because *it is enjoined by God.* Whether we agree with what God has said, He's said it anyway; and whether we like what God has done, He's done it anyway. Our attitudes don't alter His actions! He has instituted authority structures to include sinful humans, so they (the structures) are not perfect and will not always do what they are supposed to do. Nevertheless, Scripture teaches that God set people in authority and requires us to be submissive to them.

Secondly, submission has been *ingrained by the Holy Spirit.* Remember in the first chapter of the Epistle we were told to be "obedient children," and shown that the work of the Trinity in our lives is designed to produce obedience. This whole concept of obedience runs through the pages of Spirit-inspired Scripture and Spirit-taught principle. So whenever the Spirit works He ingrains a healthy attitude towards obedience and authority.

Thirdly, submission was *enacted by our Lord Jesus*. The very tone, the very fiber of His life on earth among us was one of acknowledging authority. Right at the end of His life He prayed, "My Father, if it is possible, may this cup be taken from me. Yet not as I will, but as you will" (Matt. 26:39). The cross was an acknowledging of the Father's final and ultimate authority. Christians, therefore, not only understand authority in principle and practice but have begun to develop submissive spirits and a willingness to respond to God-ordained authority.

But there is one big "but" here. There is another way of approaching the subject of authority as addressed by Peter—and that is to measure what he did alongside what he said! Peter is before the authorities. They are interrogating him:

"Is it true that you have been preaching?"

"Yes."

"And is it true that you have been preaching in the name of Christ?"

"Yes."

"And is it true that you have been forbidden to do so?"

"Yes."

"Therefore you admit that having been forbidden to preach in the name of Christ you have now been doing it?"

"Yes."

This is the man who said, "Submit to every authority." Peter's problem was as old as the rocks of Galilee. When God says one thing and the authorities ordained by God contradict it, what do you do? His answer to the authorities was straightforward. "We must obey God rather than men." (See Acts 4:1-21.) Authorities instituted by God are there to reward those who do good and to punish those who do evil and to maintain peace and order so that people may live productively and for God in a sinful society. But when the government itself becomes evil and opposes the good it is supposed to support, there is a major failure of authority and the Christian knows it. When the government actually contravenes the law of God and tells people to do that which God has flatly forbidden, the Christian recognizes that the ultimate authority is God's.

We must be very careful at this point because popular attitudes at the present time encourage insubordination. It is normal to answer the referee back, to downgrade authority figures, to evade taxes, to rebel against parents. Peter's principle must not be regarded as an excuse for insubordination. It is a simple escape clause to be used only when there is a clear conflict between what God has said and what divinely-ordained authority tells us to do.

A young woman came to me and said, "I've become a Christian and the Bible says I should submit to my husband as the one who is the authority in my family. My husband is opposed to Christianity but he keeps reminding me that Christians submit. He told me that he wanted me to go to a wife-swapping party with him, but I didn't want to go. But he told me to submit to his authority! I talked to some Christian friends and they said I should obey, that they would pray and God would deliver me. But when I found myself in bed with somebody else's husband I realized that God didn't deliver me." What a tragedy that her well-meaning friends had such an inadequate understanding of the biblical teaching on submission to authority! Peter goes on to talk about:

Liberty and the Christian Citizen

With superb balance he commands, "Live as free men, but do not use your freedom as a cover-up for evil; live as servants of God" (1 Pet. 2:16). Living like free men is a very popular subject in our day and generation. It shows itself in moral standards, political stances and personal priorities. The common desire appears to be that restrictions be taken away so we can enjoy what we fondly imagine to be liberty. We don't seem to understand that to take away limits and restrictions does not produce liberty; it simply promotes anarchy.

To understand liberty properly as Christians we must first look into *the law of liberty* (see Jas. 1:25). This expression appears to couple two mutually contradictory terms—law and liberty. But, contrary to many heady theories, we must recognize that if we're going to be free we must come under the law (or principle) of freedom that is contained in the Word of God. This means, among other things, that we recognize Christ the Lord as Liberator, Redeemer and Saviour from the consequences and the dominion of sin.

It is in the deliverance of Christ that there is freedom; but it is under His Lordship that His freedom is offered—freedom from things that hinder and mar and spoil us as individuals and wreck us as a society, but freedom only according to the principles of God's Word. Christians know this and refuse to be taken in by all the talk about individual rights to absolute freedom to do whatever they wish. They look into all the movements—

whether freedom, liberation, revolutionary or reactionary—through the filter of the Word of God. Therein, and only therein, they discover the perfect law of liberty, which allows real freedom.

Secondly, Christians recognize *the limits of liberty* because they know that human beings were created dependent and interdependent. Dependency and interdependency are clearly God-ordained limits upon our human liberty. We are free to breathe but not without air, to feed but not without food, to relate but not without relationships. All this God determined, and there is no escaping His limits. Liberty, therefore, is found not in the absence of limits but in living joyfully and freely and submissively within God-ordained limits.

Thirdly, we need to recognize the nature of *the life of liberty*. Peter says we are not to "use [our] freedom as a cover-up for evil; [but to] live as servants of God" (1 Pet. 2:16). Isn't it interesting that the words *servant* (or slave) and *liberty* appear in the same context? He is telling us that our liberty is exercised properly when we *freely* submit ourselves to His Lordship, *freely* commit ourselves to His service, and *freely* accept the role of disciple. When this is done we know the truth of Jesus' words, if "you . . . know the truth . . . the truth will set you free" (John 8:32). A look into the perfect law of liberty reveals that liberty has its limits and that true liberty is found in submission to the Lord Jesus and acceptance of a life of discipleship and service.

The abuse of liberty produces excesses of liberty. That is why Peter warns that we must not use our liberty "as a cover-up [or cloak] for evil." It's very easy to say, "I'm free so I can do what I like," without realizing that "what I like" is fleshly and sinful and, therefore, my "freedom" has become evil. Economic liberty can produce the evil of greed, political liberty the evil of pride, religious liberty the evil of license.

Liberty can also be an excuse for laziness. I often pass through Miami airport, pushing my way through thousands of people from all over South and Central America and North America. But among the crowds I always see some people I know, no matter what time of day or night. There is a girl there who is about 6'2". There is a little pimply youth with a hairpiece. They sell books, they give away flowers and expect a donation. They have blank eyes—they are members of a cult! They are trying to earn their salvation. That's why they are there and that's why they work! Now evangelical Christians know salvation is a gift. They are "free from works" as a means of salvation; but unfortunately, compared to the cults, we often use our liberty as an excuse for laziness.

What then is the exercise of liberty? Peter tells us quite simply, "Live as a slave of the living God," which means, freely choose a life of service. In freely choosing the life of service we clearly show submission to the One whose we are and whom we serve. The pagans then will enquire as we serve God and them:

"Do you have to do that?"

"No."

"Well, why do you do it?"

"Because I serve the living God and in His name I commit myself to you."

That will put the pagans on enquiry! That's why being a volunteer in the service of Jesus Christ is so challenging to a society which doesn't want to volunteer to do anything. That is why we need to underline the absolute necessity of using our liberty freely to do acts of service to the living God and to mankind.

Dignity and the Christian Citizen

"Show proper respect to everyone: Love the brotherhood of believers, fear God, honor the king" (1 Pet. 2:17), says the apostle. The Christian approach to dignity is unique.

Christians respect the dignity of the individual not for any humanistic reason, but because every individual has worth because he was created by God, and Christ thought he was worth dying for. The Christian view of society is centered in the theological perception of the individual as loved by God. "Proper respect" for everyone is based on this noble premise and demands the highest possible regard for the dignity of God's creation.

Secondly, the Christian has a high view of the dignity of the brotherhood of believers because it was purchased with Christ's own blood. The church of Jesus Christ is deeply engraved on His heart and therein lies its dignity. It is very easy to be critical of the church because it is made up exclusively of sinners. Anyone who cannot find flaws in the fabric of the faithful has lost his critical faculties! But if we rip to shreds the church of Jesus Christ we are ripping Christ's bride, and if we spend time accusing the brethren we are doing the devil's work. Therefore, if we're going to have a proper view of our citizenship among the pagans we must not join the pagans in ripping the church to shreds. They may have that right but we don't because we understand the dignity of the church of Jesus Christ.

We also must have a tremendous sense of the dignity of the Lord Himself. That is expressed in the term "fear God." We know that from Him we come and to Him we go and through Him and for Him we exist. Without Him we are nothing and have nothing so we have a great sense of His majesty and we come into His presence with a great sense of His awesome dignity.

Then there is the dignity of the king (or the president) as ordained by God. Whether we voted for him or against him is irrelevant. Whether we like his policies or his profile or not is of little consequence. But as the king, or the president, he is part of the authority structure ordained by God. He may be good, bad or indifferent, but his office has significance and dignity because of God's ordination. And Christians, knowing this, avoid pagan excuses of abuse of his dignity.

Christians have a long tradition of recognizing the dignity of the poor, the underprivileged and the oppressed and have taken a stand on their behalf. They have not fallen into the trap of seeing only physical and social need, because their understanding of man as spiritual being with eternal consequence has demanded a commitment to spiritual needs as well. Evangelical Christianity, at its best, has maintained a fine balance in the area of due regard for human dignity.

Respect for the fellowship of believers will not be shown by avoiding it and criticizing it, but by getting into it and building it up! If we're going to show proper respect for the Lord or, as Peter tells us, "fear God," then it means we reverence Him, we have a high regard for Him. We take Him seriously, we take to heart what He says and we seek to bring our lives into line with what He has commanded, living gladly in terms of what He has promised.

I read recently about a seventeenth-century German theologian and pastor called Herman August Franck. Pastor Franck had such a concern for the preaching of Christ to the underprivileged and the poor that he built orphanages, schools and homes for the wayward and the lost. He was deeply involved in the lives of these people and, in the name of Christ, he sought to uphold their dignity. He loved the brotherhood of believers and was deeply involved in the authority structures of his society and, above all, he feared God and served the Lord Jesus. Eventually all the institutions he founded and all the ministries he initiated fell into the hands of the Communists when his country was taken over. But the esteem in which he was held was such that they preserved his work. They pay for the upkeep of his library and they maintain his buildings. While they reject his God and while they refuse to bow the knee to his Lord they can't deny what Pastor Franck did.

If you go to East Germany and see what is left of the ministry of Herman August Franck you'll see a remarkable tribute to a man who understood authority and liberty and dignity and, because he did, lives on in the midst of a pagan society two or three centuries after his decease. He proved that Peter was right when Peter said, "By doing good [we] should silence the ignorant talk of foolish men." The word *silence* there means "to muzzle a yapping dog." We're called to be spiritual in a secular world, citizens of heaven living down here in this world. We're called to be servants and disciples of the living Christ in a world that is fundamentally pagan. And in living as we're called to, in the power of the Spirit, we put to silence the yapping of a lot of people ignorant of God.

ELEVEN

INJUSTICE
1 Peter 2:18-25

It is probable that a high percentage of the early Christians were slaves. We have an understandable and natural abhorrence for the institution of slavery, and we thank God that it was overthrown and that the Christian church took the lead in dealing with this ultimate injustice.

The Lord Jesus said practically nothing about slavery and His disciples were no more vocal than He, but that does not mean that they were not doing something about it.

It has been estimated that there were approximately 870,000 people living in Rome around the beginning of the first century and, in a 30-year period, 500,000 of that 870,000 people were slaves who got their freedom. Imagine the strain on an economy where suddenly 57 percent of the population is "let go"—homeless, jobless and resourceless—dumped on a society with no way of caring for them. That is a picture of the slavery situation in New Testament times.

Maybe that is why there was no attempt on the part of the early Christians to overthrow the system. But there was a deep commitment to ministering to both slaves and slave owners so that relationships could change dramatically. This Christian approach is not without relevance today because some of us, perhaps, think we're slaves to kitchen sinks or we're the property of bloodsucking employers, and we need to know how to handle grave injustice.

Injustice and the Extreme of Slavery

In New Testament times a slave was simply treated as property. His feelings, his rights and his personhood were of little concern. He was regarded as chattel, a piece of property, beef, brawn and muscle, the means of getting a job done rather than a person of eternal consequence. Aristotle, who said many enlightened things, was well below his best when he said, "Masters and slaves have nothing in common; a slave is simply a living tool."

We may wonder how people became slaves. A high percentage of them were, of course, born in slavery. Many of them were prisoners of war who had been captured in overseas campaigns. Some of them had gotten into such financial straits that their only resources were the lives of their wives, children and selves; so when they went bankrupt they sold themselves as slaves to creditors. (This practice was banned in Rome in 326 BC). Then there were those who were actually bred as slaves. Their parents had been "mated" by unscrupulous owners. This kind of slavery was common at the time Peter was writing.

However, there was a brighter side to the situation. Many slaves were being granted their freedom, but not always for altruistic reasons! The Romans had a problem manning their armies, and when they couldn't get volunteers they released slaves and immediately drafted them. Talk about out of the frying pan into the fire! Just prior to Peter's time of writing, half a million slaves had been released to Rome itself; many of them had been sent off to the colonies against their desires. When the Romans wanted to colonize an area and nobody wanted to go, they simply released the slaves and made them establish the new colonies. Some gained their freedom when the master died. The freed slave wore a speckled hat, and lots of speckled hats at the funeral helped to eulogize the deceased!

Taxes were based on the number of people in the household, and some owners didn't want to pay taxes on old worn-out slaves, so they kicked them out. Terrible injustice was the lot of a high percentage of the populace in Peter's day, and the problem was real in the small congregations of believers.

Slavery was accepted under certain circumstances in Israel in Old Testament times, but it was regulated by very strict rules. Hebrews could not have Hebrews as slaves. They could have people from other countries as slaves but they had to release them on the seventh year. Then, of course, there was the great year of Jubilee, which was specially important for slaves. The beautiful Liberty Bell in Philadelphia bears the inscription, "Proclaim liberty throughout the land." That is a superb example of taking a verse out of its context and making it say exactly what it isn't saying. That quotation has nothing to do with the American Revolution or the French Revolution; it comes from Leviticus 25 which explains that on the fiftieth year, the year of Jubilee, all slaves were to be liberated. This was certainly not what many of the founding fathers had in mind in Philadelphia! So slaves in ancient Israel had more grounds for hope than in Colonial and Revolutionary America, despite what the Liberty Bell says.

When we get into the Christian church scene we find that Peter was writing to many people who were slaves, former slaves or masters of slaves. He doesn't say to the slaves, "revolt and run away," and he doesn't say to the masters, "let them go." He tells them to start regarding each other as people of infinite worth and, therefore, build each other up, care for each other, and love each other! We all know that the system of slavery could not survive this revolutionary approach. In this way Christianity laid an axe at the root of the tree of slavery. It was by a careful, invisible revolution of love, nurture and care that people's attitudes were changed and society was rid of a blot on her countenance.

This is a powerful message for us today. The ideal situation would be where both slave and owner acted Christianly to each other while working toward a solution for the social ill in which they were both trapped. But many slaves lived in grossly unjust situations, and to them Peter wrote, "Submit yourselves to your masters with all respect, not only to those who are good and considerate, but also to those who are harsh" (1 Pet. 2:18).

We can apply this to our situation and remind ourselves that the Christian approaches injustice quite differently from other people. Peter says, categorically, "To this you were called" (v. 21). To what? The previous sentence tells us—"If you suffer for doing good and you endure it, this is commendable before God. To this you were called." The Christian attitude towards injustice means he will accept what is coming to him in all good conscience because he realizes that he was "called" to this kind of behavior. This remarkable statement is undergirded by the example of the Saviour in His reaction to injustice. "Christ suffered for you, leaving you an example, that you should follow in his steps" (v. 21). This verse has often been taken out of context and applied to all kinds of things, but its real significance is that it gives an example of how a Christian handles injustice.

Injustice and the Example of the Saviour

The irregularities of His trials. Jesus was subjected to a Hebrew trial before the Sanhedrin and a Roman trial before Pontius Pilate. Both trials were riddled with irregularities. He was captured and taken before the Sanhedrin by people who were intent on having Him put to death. But the point of the Sanhedrin trial was that justice might be done. Not only that, this particular trial was illegal because the Sanhedrin was not allowed to meet on the Sabbath or on a feast day. But Christ was tried on Passover. Capital offenses could not be tried at night, and the death penalty could not be passed until the day following the trial. Christ was sentenced to death at a night trial. Not only that, Sanhedrin trials were supposed to start with statements for the acquittal of the accused; and sometimes the evidence for acquittal was so compelling that the prosecution would not be presented. In the case of the Lord Jesus there was not even a word as to why He should be acquitted.

Then they took Him to the Roman governor because he alone had the right to pass the death penalty. In the Sanhedrin they had charged Him with blasphemy, but before Pilate the charge was altered to treason. When Pilate examined Him under that charge he said, "I find no fault in this man" (see Luke 23:4). In other words He was acquitted. At that moment Jesus should have been allowed to go free, but the judge succumbed to the threats of the crowd. He washed his hands of the whole matter knowing he was sending an innocent man to death. That was the height of injustice.

Peter, writing to slaves, reminds them that their Saviour lived and died in an unjust world and handled it well. When they hurled insults at Him He did not retaliate; when He suffered He made no threats. He responded to the situation uniquely, and Peter's thrust is that those who suffer injustice as Christians are to follow His example.

The inhumanity of His cross. Crucifixion was not a Hebrew means of execution but a Roman invention. It is interesting that the Hebrews were particularly anxious to have Him crucified. Perhaps the leaders of His opposition wanted Him to have the most humiliating death imaginable. Crucifixion to a Jew would bring the ultimate shame because the Old Testament said, "Cursed is everyone who hangs on a tree" (see Gal. 3:13; Deut. 21:23). That's what they wanted for Him, the ultimate of shame and degradation.

As He hung in shame He was confronted with the undisguised hostility of the crowds that had gathered around. They mocked and jeered at Him, intent on adding agony to ignominy. Even one who was crucified at His side turned on Him and vilified Him. Wherever He looked there was no support. His disciples had forsaken Him and fled, and as He looked up to the Father He cried from the depth of His soul, "My God, my God, why have you forsaken me?" (Matt. 27:46). All this, Peter says, portrays the awful injustice to which Christ was subjected.

The importance of His example. Instead of taking matters into His own hands He entrusted them into God's hands. Peter says, "When he suffered, he made no threats. Instead he entrusted himself to him who judges justly" (1 Pet. 2:23). When we suffer injustice we need to resist the natural impulse to take matters into our own hands and we must commend ourselves to the keeping of the One who judges justly.

We also need to notice that He endured on behalf of other people, in fact, it says in verse 21, "Christ suffered for you." Some people think that Christ was just suffering for His own actions or because of Pilate or because of the hostility of leaders of His day. But the Bible teaches that the sufferings of Christ were foreordained of God before the foundation of the world. If He had taken matters into His own hands when He was subjected to injustice He might have preserved His own position, but He would have disqualified Himself from being the means of blessing to everybody on the face of God's earth. He endured the injustice to bring blessing to others.

He was also prepared to endure the injustice because Peter tells us, "By his wounds you have been healed." In His act of submission to injustice there was potential healing for the very people who subjected Him to the injustice! As they crucified Him He prayed, "Father, forgive them, for they do not know what they are doing" (Luke 23:34). In the illegality of His trials He did not complain about injustice, in the inhumanity of His cross He did not retaliate against the ignominy. But He committed His affairs into the hand of God as He looked upon the concerns of others, and He knew that the wounds in His own body would bring healing to many.

"To this you were called," says the apostle to the slaves in the churches. Not that he minimized the injustice of the slaves' situation. He didn't approve of it and he didn't agree with it, but he encouraged them to handle injustice properly, and in the end justice would be done and innumerable people would be blessed.

Injustice and the Experience of the Shepherd

We now need to consider practically how these powerful truths about the Christian response to injustice should be handled.

We should recognize the root of injustice. Peter points out that Christ, as He was suffering under injustice, was dealing with sins. So let's start by calling injustice by its proper name—sin. I'm not just quoting the Bible at this moment, I'm also quoting good old Abraham Lincoln. In 1854 he said, "Slavery is grounded in the selfishness of man's nature, opposition to it in his love of justice."

Lincoln saw in injustice the selfishness of man's nature; Peter saw the sinfulness of man's nature. A Christian looks at a sinner not as a rotten apple, but as a person for whom Christ died; and therein lies the totally different response to injustice. If we regard injustice as the product of people that we hate, we will retaliate and produce a big conflict. If we, as Christians, regard injustice as the product of the sinful nature, we will call the unjust sinners and take steps to express concern for them. Slaves should submit to masters who treat them badly because their masters are proving they are sinners by their unjust actions; and slaves have been known to lead sinful masters to repentance!

We need to return to the Shepherd. Peter says, "You were like sheep going astray, but now you have returned to the Shepherd and Overseer of your souls" (1 Pet. 2:25). God chose, of all the animals in creation, to call human beings "sheep." He could have compared us to strong oxen or noble horses or even cute kittens; but He preferred to call us sheep. Sheep have an inbuilt waywardness, a remarkable capacity for going wrong. When left to their own devices sheep will foul things up; but when given a shepherd it's amazing how they change! Our world is full of injustice because wayward sheep, doing their own thing, have rejected the Shepherd. Our society is suffering because it is made up of people who disregard the Shepherd's leading and are heaping injustice upon injustice and producing retaliation against retaliation. But in the midst of it there are some people who have chosen to return to the Shepherd, to reject waywardness and to commit themselves to the Overseer of their souls. When the Overseer, our Example, takes over, His impetus begins to produce reactions to injustice similar to His own.

We need to respond to the call. As we have seen, Peter reminds the believers of their call—not to mediocrity or to conformity, but to uniqueness and submissiveness. This idea of "calling" was powerful in Peter's thinking because it was only because of God's "call" that he was an apostle and not a fisherman, a winner of the souls of men rather than a fisher of the denizens of the deep. Equally powerful to him was the calling to distinctive behavior in the teeth of injustice.

We need to relate to the Cross. Peter wrote, "He himself bore our sins in his body on the tree" (not so that we might have our sins forgiven and live happily everafter, but) "so that we might die to sins and live for righteousness." Look at it this way: when Jesus died on the cross for sin He showed His true feelings about sin, which contrast sharply with our tendency to take sin lightly once sins have been forgiven. Peter insists that when we identify with the Lord Jesus we begin to adopt His attitude towards sin. We die to what He died to and live for what He lives for. Our retaliation against injustice might be as sinful as the injustice imposed upon us in the first place. Once we are conscious of its sinfulness and our stance on sin, our lives must be committed to a new view of injustice in all its forms not least in our reaction to it.

To follow the example of Christ when faced with injustice must not become a noble, empty phrase or a futile soul-destroying exercise. The only way I know to avoid both extremes is to bear in mind continually that He is not only Example but also Enabler.

I once took giant steps in a field of new snow and challenged my small children to "walk as I walked"—to follow my example. They failed for obvious reasons until I placed my hands under their armpits, their feet on mine, and they discovered my abilities flowing through them, to their intense delight.

I know of nothing more delightful than reacting uniquely as Christ did because He showed me that *I ought,* and shows me, through His power, that *I can.*

TWELVE

MARRIAGE IN FOCUS
1 Peter 3:1-7

Often when we are under pressure we lash out at people, and our interpersonal relationships disintegrate. This is particularly tragic because the relationships we destroy at such times are designed to be a great strength for tough times. They are not intended to be the target at which we can lash out when the going gets tough.

Marriage is a "divine institution." It is something that God has ordained for the well-being of the individual and society. A solid, stable marriage can and should be a tremendous resource in difficult times; but it is a sad commentary on our society that marriages are fracturing under stress instead of nourishing those who find life difficult. It is important to note that Peter takes time to write about marriage in the context of his concern for believers.

Applying the Principles of Christian Marriage
Sound marriages which survive stress, like

solid buildings, are built on firm foundations—
God-given principles.

*The principle of spiritual equality—seeing we
are heirs together.* "Husbands," Peter says, "in the
same way be considerate as you live with your
wives, and treat them with respect as the weaker
partner and as heirs with you of the gracious gift
of life" (v. 7). We must see ourselves as "heirs
together." Men, you are to regard yourselves, if you
are believers, as heirs of God and joint heirs with
Christ. You are heirs to all that Christ is heir to,
which means one day you will share the glory of
God and will live for all eternity in the presence of
the living God! Men, that's exciting, but don't forget your wife is just as much an heir! You are heirs
together.

Husbands and wives are heirs together of the
grace of God. Paul said, "By the grace of God I am
what I am" (1 Cor. 15:10), suggesting that if there
was anything of significance, anything of importance, anything of relevance in his life it was
attributable to the undeserved intervention of
God. Peter insists that husbands see their wives in
this light, as inheritors of God's grace.

Men, we are also heirs of life, not just life down
here, but life eternal; and both husband and wife
share the exalted position—a life of eternal and
spiritual equality. Christian marriage rests on the
solid basis of spiritual equality. Two people who
are heirs of God and joint heirs with Christ, with
identical eternal expectations, attributing everything to the grace of God, having become recipients of life eternal, sharing their lives—that's the
basis!

In the days in which Peter was writing, women
were still regarded as property, little better than

slaves. The New Testament teaching on the place of women must be seen in this context, and we will realize what a positive, liberating effect it had on the women and what joy it could bring to marriage. By insisting that men see women in Christ, marriage was elevated into a new and glorious position, which we must affirm in our day.

The principle of spiritual equality—saying our prayers together. Peter tells his readers to behave in a certain way "so that nothing will hinder your prayers" (1 Pet. 3:7). He assumes that they believe in prayer because they believe that God rules in their affairs. They relate to Him all their concerns and problems and plans. They pray about their children, their finances, their jobs, their homes and their futures. Everything is bathed in prayer because we're heirs together and everything has eternal divine significance.

Prayer is also an indication of gratitude. People who pray are people who praise. People who praise are people who understand the grace of God and respond to it in gratitude. Bickering and fighting pervade the atmosphere of many a marriage, but not a Christian marriage where there is an understanding of spiritual equality and reality. There is an understanding that we're saying prayers together because we are united in gratitude to God. Many couples don't need to get into a lot of marriage counseling; all they need to do is introduce these two aspects of spiritual equality into their relationship.

The principle of spiritual equality—sharing our cares together. This is a beautiful aspect of togetherness. God, having created man, decided it was not good for man to be alone; so He made woman. By bringing woman into man's life He

introduced an immediate and unique resource—
what the old Bibles call "a helpmeet." She was
somebody who would be utterly supportive and
totally ideal for the situation. Standing by her
man, standing alongside him through thick and
thin, she would be what he could never be and do
what he could never do. And while she was sup-
porting and encouraging him, he was doing the
same for her—sharing and caring for each other,
together.

*The principle of sexual mutuality—mutual
comfort.* Peter writes in verse 7, "Husbands, in the
same way be considerate as you live with your
wives." The Greek word for "live with your wives" is
most interesting. In contemporary English we
sometimes talk about people "living together," but
what we mean is that they share the same bed.
Peter's word has the same emphasis and suggests
"living together" with particular reference to sexual mutuality, the sharing of bodies which is an
integral part of marriage. This principle must be
carefully built into marriage because it is an exercise in mutuality. *Together* is the important word!
When we come together, sexually or otherwise, we
can reasonably expect mutual comfort. A man in
trouble in the office, if he has built his marriage
properly, can come home and instead of being
nagged he will be comforted. But at the same time
his wife who has had a horrendous day can reasonably expect some understanding and support
too. There must be mutual comfort.

*The principle of sexual mutuality—mutual
companionship.* Marriage partners must be good
friends who enjoy each other's company. My wife
and I, after 23 years of marriage, are better friends
than we have ever been. We both travel extensively

but we don't miss an opportunity to be together. Recently in the space of a few weeks I was in Guatemala, Hong Kong, Hawaii and the Bahamas. When Jill picked me up at the airport, after one period apart from each other, we went out and leisurely ate a pizza and talked! That pizza, frankly, was the best part of the trip because it was an experience of mutual comforting and mutual companionship.

The principle of sexual mutuality—mutual completion. The marriage relationship is intended to portray the relationship between Christ and His church. Paul tells us that the church is "the fullness of him" (Eph. 1:23); that means it completes Him! Christ doesn't have a physical body but He does have the church, so in this sense it fills up what is lacking. Men need to admit that there are great gaping holes in their masculine experience and God brought forth woman to complete what is lacking. In the same way women, whatever they are being told at the present time, need to admit to the major deficiencies which only a man can fill.

You may say, "I thought there was something sexual about this passage!" There is, but it is imperative that we see that sex is not just the coupling of bodies but is intimately related to the comforting of spirits, the companionship of persons, and the completion of whole personalities. One of the great tragedies of our contemporary society is that we have divorced the giving of bodies in the sex act from the giving of ourselves in mutuality. We have divorced the physical and sexual from the reality of the psychological and the spiritual, and have brought untold disaster into our society. In a healthy marriage there will be a "living together" in the fullest sense of the word.

Sexuality brings mutual comfort, demonstrates mutual companionship and develops mutual completion in a unique manner. It is absolutely fundamental that it be there, but it is also important that husbands should "be considerate" in this particularly precious and sensitive area of marriage.

Bearing in mind the prevailing attitudes of men to women at the time Peter wrote the Epistle we can see again the uplifting and ennobling impact the Christian message had on first-century society. It goes without saying that the twenty-first century will need a similar uplifting if twentieth-century erosion of human sexuality and marriage continues.

One extreme we have in our society is that there are people who want their sex without marriage. On the other hand there are those who would like marriage without sex. Neither will do—as Peter clearly enunciated—for true mutuality is a sharing of the whole person with a whole person.

The principle of physical disparity. Returning to verse 7 we read, "Husbands,. . . live with your wives, and treat them with respect as the weaker partner." In our modern society, where women are standing up and being counted, the fur begins to fly when the "weaker vessel" is introduced! There is no suggestion in Scripture that the woman is spiritually inferior. She is spiritually equal as we have seen. Those of us who have been to school know that the woman is definitely not intellectually inferior. Woman is most definitely not morally inferior; in fact when it comes down to moral issues the women often have a keener sense of what is right than the men. And when it comes to sheer courage my observation as a pastor is that when there are problems in marriage, 95 percent of the time it's the women who have the courage to deal with it, and the men chicken out!

When we talk about the women being the "weaker vessel" I believe we're talking about physical limitations. No doubt I will be challenged to run a marathon now by some of the girls who have done it, or challenged as I was recently by a beautiful young female athlete to putt the shot! Of course there are exceptions to this rule, but it is generally true despite specific exceptions. This means that the husband must build in the principle of physical disparity and demonstrate it by a sensitivity to his wife's physical limitations and also be aware of the emotional pressures that those physical limitations bring. Many marriages experience difficulties because the wife is expected to run the home, raise the kids, hold down a job, look like a dream, be a gourmet cook and perform like a sexual gymnast. Christian men, particularly, need to build into their marriages an understanding of physical disparity, and treat their wives accordingly.

One day Peter said to the Lord, "We have given up a lot, Lord. What is going to happen to us?" And the Lord said, "Anybody who has given up home or mother or father or children or wife for my sake and the gospel will not be forgotten. Don't you worry about it." (See Matt. 19:27-29.) In short, the Lord Jesus told Peter that being a disciple would make great demands on home life, marriage, wives and children. The church was founded by men and women who understood and accepted this worthy call of discipleship. However, in 1 Corinthians 9, Paul, talking about the rights of an apostle, claimed he had as much right to take a wife on his journey as Peter! In the early days of ministry Peter was told he would have to go away from home and be lonely and live apart from wife and family for periods of time. Later on he obviously took his wife with him. I wonder why that was? Perhaps somewhere along the way Peter's wife said, "Peter, I've had it with this arrangement!" And he said, "Alright, you come with me!" It may be that he was sensitive to her limitations and nurtured his marriage and his ministry. If that is not what happened, it should have happened!

The principle of practical authority. I have dealt at some length with the latter part of this section of Scripture because I feel that, in our society where there is Christian teaching on marriage, there is usually an inordinate emphasis on the woman's role with particular reference to her submission!

Having taken time to talk about the man's role I feel it's safe now to go to verse 1. "Wives, in the same way be submissive to your husbands." As we have seen, the Christian in all areas of his experience recognizes authority. The Christian understands submission because he acknowledges Christ as Lord, which spells submission. Bearing all this in mind Peter instructs wives to demonstrate this attitude to their husbands.

Authority structures are necessary in all areas of society including marriage. We have noted that male and female have equality, enjoy mutuality and recognize disparity. But everyone knows that when groups of more than one person live in equality not everybody can make the necessary decisions, so when they have to be made, somebody must take charge. The buck has to stop somewhere. And God says in marriage the buck stops with the male, who has authority over the female. Some wives will claim that they are better at making decisions than their man. That may well be true, but they should remember that their decisiveness led them to an indecisive husband, so maybe they are not so good at deciding after all!

Seriously, when there is genuine equality of male and female, when a decision has to be made there will be mutual sharing and double impact; and on the rare occasions that agreement is not reached the man must decide and the woman must submit to the decision. In my marriage I remember only three occasions when I had to "put my foot down"! Jill says four, but I conveniently forget the fourth because I was wrong! Where there is mutuality there is a pulling together, a building up together and a mutual giving to each other, so decisions will usually be unanimous. When they aren't, and somebody has to make an awkward decision, the other person will be supportive because equality and mutuality are the bases of marriage. These are the principles which must be built into Christian marriages and men have the special responsibility to see that they are in operation.

On reading this section of the Epistle it would be easy to assume that women need six times as much instruction as men, because he addresses six verses to wives and only one to husbands! This was not the case! In the early days of the church it was not uncommon for a pagan woman to become a Christian without her husband making a similar commitment. But if the man became a believer he would require, as head of the family, that the wife join him in the faith. It was not unusual to find a marriage between a pagan man and a Christian woman, but most unlikely between a pagan woman and a Christian man.

Christians, as we have seen, were confronting tough times when Peter wrote to them, and he was eager to point out the great resource of a Christian marriage. But such a resource was not available to the Christian partner in a mixed marriage, so Peter has detailed instructions for them. He makes it clear that her prime objective is to win her husband over to Christ, both for his eternal benefit and also for their mutual blessing. The way she is to embark on this task is to "be submissive to" her husband, even those who "flagrantly disobey the word" (this is the literal meaning of Peter's words).

Careful attention to behavior is the first emphasis. Earnest new believers find it hard to serve when their unbelieving spouses don't want to hear about Christ; but they must learn the art of practicing quietness instead of picking quarrels, and learning cooperation rather than loving confrontation. Christianity should be highly *visible*, not horribly *vocal*.

Careful attention to beauty is the second emphasis. Unbelieving men will love Peter's words here because they will save themselves thousands of dollars! Look at this: "Your beauty should not come from outward adornment, such as braided hair and the wearing of gold jewelry and fine clothes." There is no reason to assume that Peter was opposed to feminine beauty but he certainly had no time for Christian women whose beauty was exclusively external. His principle here is to seek an expressive character, not expensive clothes, an inner attitude, not outer adornment.

Careful attention to bravery is the third

emphasis. Using the illustration of Sarah, who "obeyed Abraham," presumably when he required her to do things that would normally produce panic, Peter draws attention to the fact that many women in difficult marriages will need to be courageous and consistent if they are to achieve for the one they love the greatest imaginable good. If over a period of time pagan husbands see a change of behavior that is positive, and a new beauty that is not just cosmetic, and sheer bravery that they know deep down in their hearts is superior to their own, there is a real possibility that new marriages will result as new men are born.

There is, however, another factor. Peter says that this kind of wife's behavior "is of great worth in God's sight." A similar word of encouragement to that which he gave the slaves—"this is commendable before God" (2:20), which is the same idea.

The best way to evaluate a marriage, Peter says, is to ask the question, "Is our marriage commending itself to God?" In addition, this kind of marriage is part of the call to "live such good lives among the pagans that, though they accuse you of doing wrong, they may see your good deeds and glorify God on the day he visits [you]" (2:12). Good Christian marriages have great worth in God's sight and great value in pagan society.

THIRTEEN

LOVING LIFE
1 Peter 3:8-12

A considerable body of theological opinion believes that the quotation from Psalm 34 in 1 Peter 3:10-12 was either adapted as a Christian hymn, in the first century, or became part of the primitive catechism. Either way it is a beautiful passage of Scripture, and the early believers memorized it in order that it might become an integral part of their thinking.

The theme is "loving life." There are different ways of looking at life. We can detest it, tolerate it or absolutely love it. We should ask ourselves what needs to be built into our days that we might feel, before God, that they are "good days." I think there are three things that we can draw from this passage of Scripture.

The Place of Belief
What we believe is fundamental to the lives we live. Many people seem to think it doesn't matter what you believe just so long as you believe it. Oth-

ers require only sincerity of belief; but the world is full of sincere people who agree they were sincerely wrong!

Belief about the existence of the Lord is of primary importance. Some believe that God is and the rest believe that God isn't, but everybody believes something! Those who believe that God exists find in Him the focal point, the center, the fundamental basis of existence. Those who believe that God does not exist must find a substitute center and basis of their existence.

Peter has built into his life a belief that the Lord is real. Not only that, he understands some specific things about the Lord. For example, "The eyes of the Lord are on the righteous and his ears are attentive to their prayer, but the face of the Lord is against those who do evil" (v. 12). There are things that God is for and there are things that God is against. How does Peter know this? Because God has revealed Himself in His Word. He revealed in the ancient psalm that He is the God of reality and the God of righteousness. What we believe about God being the essence of righteousness and that which is the opposite of Him being the essence of wrongness will determine the whole of life. When right and wrong, good and evil are defined in terms of Him, in the midst of a society which, having chosen to believe He does not exist, have made their own standards, the difference of Christian thought and behavior is obvious.

He is also the God of relationships, as is shown by His choice of the name *Jehovah* (translated "Lord"). Jehovah is the name that God chose to use to reveal Himself as a God who desires personal, intimate, deep relationships with people. This is one of the most magnificent things about divine revelation. God is not an impersonal force, a theological concept, the unmoved mover or the uncaused cause, but He is one who freely chooses to introduce Himself to people so that they might live in an intimate relationship with Him which the Bible calls "knowing" Him. "To know Him is to love Him" becomes much more than a hackneyed phrase reserved for eulogies when applied to Jehovah. And to love Him is to obey Him by living life His way.

Belief about the experience of life is also crucial. Peter is quite straightforward about life. He says it's tough, it's hard and difficult; but despite that we should love it. Peter is a firm believer that God has given us all things richly to enjoy. It's interesting to notice that Peter, in quoting King David, aligns himself with the king who believed that life should be good, that life should be loved. But the writer of Ecclesiastes, who had similar opportunities and experiences to those of King David, came to an exactly opposite conclusion. In contrast to David's "I love life," he wrote, "I hated life." "Vanity of vanities" was his cynical summary of life. Meaninglessness of meaninglessness—everything is meaningless! What we believe about life, whether it is to be enjoyed in relationship with God or endured in a maelstrom of meaninglessness, will affect every aspect of life.

Belief about the exercise of liberty. The Bible is replete with instructions and commands, and this passage has its fair share. If we accept that they are God's instructions to people it is a reasonable assumption that God intends us to obey them. But in giving us the ability to obey, God gave us the liberty to disobey Him. A fundamental of human experience is that there is built-in liberty.

It is something which God has ordained. But this liberty, depending on what we believe about it, can be either an untold blessing or an unmitigated blight.

It is as important that we look into what we believe about liberty as it is for us to look into what we believe about everything else. For instance, when the Lord, through Peter, says, "Live in harmony with one another" (1 Pet. 3:8), He knows perfectly well that some will produce more discord than harmony and be perfectly content with what they are doing. When He says, "be sympathetic" He knows some will choose not to be sympathetic and when He says, "be humble" He knows that some people will say, "That is the worst thing you can do—if you want to get ahead you have to promote yourself!" In short, when the Bible gives us instructions, imperatives, and commands it presupposes our freedom to obey or to disobey. But before the decision to obey or not, there has to be an ability to discern the options and consequences, and God has given that freedom too. What we believe about freedoms will have monumental impact on whether we live "good days" or bad.

The Place of Behavior

Behavior is inexplicably bound up in belief. Considerable research into human behavior patterns is being pursued at this time. Contemporary Christians need never fear honest, scientific discovery—but underline "honest" and "scientific"! Some "scientific" work is dishonest in the extreme because of its unfair, unwarranted presuppositions. Christians should be aware of this but equally aware of the folly of denying the helpful insights into human behavior being gained through secular research. Christian belief based on the ancient Book inspired by God and "scientific discovery" of the wonders of God's creation are experiences of truth. The two should enrich each other.

One of the things that is rather obvious is that our *behavior is clearly related to our convictions*—what we believe thoroughly will make us feel deeply, which will lead to distinct behavior. For example, in verses 10 and 11, Peter quotes the psalmist, who says that if we're going to enjoy life and "see good days" we must "turn from evil and do good." It's one thing to turn from evil and leave it at that, but the person who really believes that evil is evil should believe also that the opposite of evil should be embraced. In other words, there is real conviction about evil and about good. It will not just be the avoiding of evil because it's nasty and might hurt us, but the "doing of good" to counter evil in others' lives.

Behavior is also related to circumstances. Some circumstances are basically agreeable. For example, verse 8 suggests a most agreeable situation where everybody is living in harmony with everybody! Everybody is sympathetic, everybody loves his brothers, everybody is compassionate, everybody is humble! Living in such circumstances would no doubt affect our behavior, but we can only guess because it is unlikely we have experienced it!

On the other hand we may find ourselves in a situation where there are all kinds of evil and insult—tongues saying rotten things and lips spewing deceitful speech. There is much that is grossly unfair, unjust and inequitable, and we suffer because of it and are affected by it. But Peter knows how circumstances can affect behavior, yet he insists there ought to be a dynamic in our lives attributable to the resurrection life of Christ that allows us to transcend circumstances rather than be consumed by circumstances. How we handle our circumstances and what we do about our convictions determine how we behave, and this decides whether or not we come up with a life we love and days that are good.

Behavior is also related to choices. When Peter says, "Finally," and then goes on for two more chapters, he is not betraying a common preacher's problem! *Finally* really means "in summary." He has given a lot of ideas and concepts to different groups but now he says, "Now in summary, all of you . . ." Everybody must now make some choices.

We must decide to live in harmony with one another. The word means literally "to share a mind-set." Some people think that when Christians live in harmony they are in agreement on every point. This is incorrect! There is no hope of Christians coming to agreement on politics or economics, organizational structures, policies, objectives and strategies. They are not expected to do this, but they are required to develop the same mind-set and share the same attitude. That's the key!

One day Peter decided the Lord Jesus needed an agent. He interposed his considerable bulk between the Lord Jesus and Jerusalem. And the Lord Jesus got rather upset and said, "Out of my sight, Satan!" That's getting upset! Then He added, "You do not have in mind the things of God, but the things of men" (Matt. 16:23). Now the word *mind* is the same word *harmony* that Peter uses in 1 Peter 3:8, and I've got a feeling he had some nasty vibes as he wrote it. He remembered when his mind-set was way off from the Lord Jesus and he had to make some decisions to get it in line. In the same way he asks for Christian choices to be made. We must stop persuading each other to have our own mind-set, and all decide that the attitude and mind-set of the Lord Jesus is that which is right, and endeavor to bring our mind-set in line with His. To develop the mind-set of Christ means submission, obedience, servant-hood and sacrifice, all of which mean great big choices, every one of which is hard.

We are also to be "sympathetic." The English word *sympathetic* is simply a Greek word slightly polished. It means, literally, "to suffer together." When we become aware of suffering we are confronted with choices. When we see the man in the ditch we may say "tut-tut" and keep going. Or we can go over and look at him and say, "If he had put out he wouldn't be in that fix," and keep going. Or we can get down in his ditch, unload our little donkey and take the risk of caring. Being sympathetic requires a choice.

We are to "love as brothers." This means "to have a mutuality of concern." The beautiful thing about Christian brotherly love is that it puts the emphasis on our common Father. Scripture teaches that we are children of God through the new birth by the Holy Spirit who imparts the life of God to us; and also we are children of God by adoption. This means that God chose to bring us into His family and give us all the benefits that are not ours by right! This privilege is not ours alone—there are others who are sons of God, and if we accept that they enjoy God as we do, there is a very real possibility we might get around to enjoying each other. When the going gets tough we tend to head for our won private little cave, build our own defenses and get ready to protect ourselves from everybody and everything. This option is not available to Christians because we are required to build the "brother" relationship.

We are to be compassionate. "Be compassionate" is a translation of a fascinating Greek word. The second part of it is a word from which we get *spleen*, and is related to *intestines*. The Greeks talked about "spleen," "bowels" and "intestines" the way we talk about "guts." A very petite, feminine young girl was once introduced to me as a "gutsy little gal." The Greeks, like us, had the idea that your spleen, intestines and guts are related to "courage." The Hebrews thought of "spleen" as determining concern and tenderheartedness. The first part of the word means "good." So "to be compassionate" means to have some "good guts," "good feelings," and "good concern" for people. Frankly, that requires good choices!

If we want to love life and see good days we *must also be "humble."* That means be "lowly-minded." Scripture tells us not to think of ourselves "more highly" than we ought to think. To be humble-minded means to have a realistic appraisal of ourselves before God. Some people are humble and proud of it. Their humility is sickening. They impose it upon you, attempting to impress you with it. They are so humble that they can go out through the door without opening it. They worm underneath and turn around to ensure that you saw it. On the other hand there is a kind of arrogance that is equally intolerable. To be lowly-minded is neither. It is to be totally realistic about who and what you are in the economy of God. And this requires a choice—will I believe what I want about myself or will I appraise myself by God's standards?

Behavior is also related to calling. Peter says, from the depths of long hard experience, "Do not repay evil with evil or insult with insult, but with blessing." Some say, "That's the craziest thing I ever heard," while others settle for, "That's hard." Of course it's hard! Have you noticed how we think the next step after "That's hard" is "It can't be serious"? The important clause to notice is "to this you were called." We're really called, at this particular point, to choose not to react naturally but to respond supernaturally through the resource of the Holy Spirit within us; but it requires a choice which we will make only if we believe that "to this [we] were called"!

So we see how calling, choices, circumstances, and convictions affect behavior. This, in turn, determines whether at the end of each day we say, "It was a good day, Lord. Thank you. Good night," or we come to the end of another day with shame. It means we get up in the morning with a keen sense of anticipation and say, "Here comes another piece of life to love" or, "Here comes another piece of life to detest."

The frosting on the cake is "the blessing of God" which Peter says we "may inherit"! God is not committed to blessing sin, nor is He so naive that He puts His stamp of approval on our disobedience! His eyes are upon those who live rightly before Him. His ears are always open to the prayers of those who love Him and respond to Him. But make no mistake about it, His face is adamantly set against those who disobey. That being the case we recognize that the blessing of God is not something that we presume upon; neither is it something that we assume is ours by rights. The blessing of God, the stamp of divine approval, comes only on lives of which He approves.

The word *blessing* (*eulogia*) is the word from which we get *eulogy* and means, literally, "to speak well of." Sometimes in a eulogy we speak so well of people after they are gone that we wonder if we got the wrong funeral. A real "eulogy," a real "blessing," a real "speaking well of" is the product of thinking highly about. To bless somebody is to think so highly of them that you speak well of them so that you pronounce good upon them. The blessing of God does this for us and ensures "good days" and a life we love because belief and behavior bring delight to Him, which means joy to us.

FOURTEEN

WHAT REALLY MATTERS
1 Peter 3:13-16

In the marines we were required to whitewash our coal buckets. To me it was the ultimate in futility, but I had to do it anyway. One day I asked an officer why it was necessary for us to do this. He replied, "We are training you to do what you're told, because one day your life may depend on your instantaneous obedience. If you get into the habit of arguing about everything you are told to do, you may find your head will be shot off while you debate an order." This is not an attempt to encourage the enforcing of stupidity, but a reminder that the way we act when tough times come is usually determined by the things that have already been built into our lives. When the tough time arrives, it is usually too late to try to build in the things that really matter.

A Matter of Confidence

Peter's question, "Who is going to harm you if you are eager to do good?" is startling to say the

least! The word *eager* in the Greek is the word
from which we get *zealous* or *zealot*. He is not
talking about doing good casually, but being sold
on doing good. Most of us feel we probably can
answer this question from bitter experience.
"Every time I've stuck my neck out to help someone they hit me on the chin, and every time I
poked my nose into something they bit it off!"

At first sight it looks as if Peter has it all wrong.
He is not saying that if we try to be good nobody
will hurt us. His statement is much more pro-
found than that. He is saying that if we are interested and committed to that which is really good,
there is nobody that can get to us. Paul makes a
number of suggestions such as "trouble, hard-
ship, persecution, famine, nakedness, danger or
sword" but affirms that none of them can "separate us from the love of God." In fact he adds, "In
all these things we are more than conquerors" (see
Rom. 8:35,37). Both Paul and Peter teach that
those people who are eager to do good are aware of
the real good that God is working in their lives
and, as a result, they are secure in Him. *This gives
us an eternal confidence.*

Some Christians in our world face tribulation,
persecution, execution. Others are concerned
about frightening spiritual powers or worry about
other creations in space getting ready to blow
planet Earth to smithereens. Many more ordinary
folks just worry about death and dying, or even life
itself. Firm confidence in God's eternal commitment does much to banish all these fears to such
an extent that it is very difficult to find out how a
believer who believes what he believes can be easily
moved. It is easy to shake somebody who doesn't
know what he believes or doesn't have any

grounds for confidence. But Peter's readers had built eternal confidence into their lives and were well prepared.

Then there is an external confidence. Peter says, "Even if you should suffer for what is right, you are blessed" (1 Pet. 3:14). There is a popular philosophy abroad in our society which has to do with pain and pleasure. The popular perception is that we have the right to escape every kind of pain and to embrace every kind of pleasure. At first sight this appears sensible enough, but a little thought will expose it as a dangerous fallacy. If we say that anything goes so long as we escape pain and enjoy pleasure, then pain and pleasure become the only determining factors. On this basis "right" is avoiding pain and enjoying pleasure and "wrong" is suffering and being unhappy. The Bible speaks very forcibly against this. Peter says you can suffer for doing right. The popular secular attitude can lead only to self-absorbed living; the latter produces people who for noble reasons and high motives are prepared to sacrifice, to share, and to suffer. Their underlying confidence in a life is beyond the immediate and their rewards beyond the obvious.

Internal confidence is another important factor. Peter's command, "In your hearts set apart Christ as Lord" is a simple but beautiful expression. When I was a boy of seven a very strange thing happened to me one Sunday morning. I was sitting absolutely alone—I wasn't reading anything, I wasn't talking to anybody. There was no influence upon me. Into my mind came the strangest thought. I jumped from my stool by the fire and asked my mother a very simple question, "Mother, how do you become a Christian?"

Using the words of Christ she said, "Behold I stand at the door and knock, and if any man hear my voice and open the door I will come in" (see Rev. 3:20). She explained to me "that Christ who died and rose again was outside my life. He was knocking on the door because He wanted to come in and it was up to me to decide whether I would open up my life to Him. If I did He promised He would come in." That day I simply invited the Christ who died for me to come and live within me, and He did. Reasoning that He is either a liar or the Truth, and convinced He wasn't a liar, the truth of the matter to me was that He had entered my life.

But Peter says more than that. Christ must be acknowledged as Lord in the heart. We must recognize Who it is whom we've invited into our hearts. The heart is like a house and Christ can be treated as we treat visitors. We may ask Him onto the porch to clean it up so the neighbors will think all is well. When the kids come along we get a little scared with the responsibility and invite Him into the nursery. Then years go by and we have trouble with the teenagers, so we get Him in the game room because we're not too sure what games they are playing! Marriage problems follow so we invite Him into the bedroom. To set Christ apart as Lord is to honor Him rather than to use Him. It means to give him the bunch of keys and ask Him to invade each area of the heart with His transforming presence.

To rightly understand the entrance of Christ into the heart we must accept the enthronement of Christ in the heart. This leads to the enjoyment of Christ in the heart. If we decide to keep part of our hearts for ourselves, when the going gets tough we are totally responsible for it. If, on the other hand, we open up our lives to His control, when the going gets tough He is in control. That's when we begin to enjoy Christ in the heart, and that's where the internal confidence comes from.

A Matter of Conviction

Confidence provokes enquiry. So Peter says we must be ready for this, stating, "Always be prepared to give an answer to everyone who asks you to give the reason for the hope that you have." When someone says, "Excuse me, you seem to be remarkably confident; would you mind very much explaining to me why you're so confident?" we must be able to explain the dynamics of our confidence. As a pastor I have often rejoiced to see people who are suffering exhibiting such courage and confidence that they have been besieged by enquiries. I have been even more delighted when they have been able to clearly articulate the convictions behind the courage. Note carefully that Peter says we should always be ready to answer anyone. That's rather all-inclusive—"always" and "anyone"! This does not mean that you should always have an answer for any question, however it is asked, on every subject. Peter mercifully limits it to questions about the hope within us! This is a great relief and a great challenge because it means that while everyone is not called to preach and be an apologist it does mean that all believers must know enough about their own experience to be able to explain it.

This requires solid conviction which comes from learning how to define the things we're talking about. Peter calls them "reasons" which will constitute a defense of a deeply-held position. An intelligent conversation requires both participants to know what the other is talking about because both may be using the same terms, but interpreting them differently.

Something more than unexplained quotations and naive testimony is required. This takes time, study and practice, which are amply repaid when we have the privilege of sharing convictions which explain the who, what and why we believe.

The way our convictions are shared is very important. I like the way Peter says, "But do it with gentleness and respect." That means we are going to have to project real concern and esteem for the people with whom we share. Serious questions must be treated with the seriousness they deserve. Many questions don't deserve a serious answer. Some people come up to me and say, "I've got a question for you"; but often I tell them, "That is not a question; it is a statement!" There are always some smart alecks who ask questions like, "Where did Cain get his wife from?" Sensing this is not coming from a serious concern, I usually answer, "I would tell you if I was Abel," or "I don't know. I wasn't invited to the wedding!" But when people come to you with genuine questions and concerns, show that you hold them in high regard by listening very intently and doing all you possibly can to help.

The way we deal with people must also show that we have high esteem for God. If we act as God's representative we assume an awesome responsibility. Explaining eternal truth to people is a burden of gigantic proportions. Jill was training a bunch of kids to go out witnessing in a supermarket. She asked me to give them a little pep talk before they embarked on their enterprise. So I went and I said, "You're going to go out to talk to people about things that are important, so be very careful because you're going to meddle with eternal souls!" My wife had a little word with me afterwards! She said, "Thanks a lot. I've worked with these kids getting them all excited about it and you come in and frighten the living daylights out of them."

I was somewhat chastened, but sharing convictions about Christ is more than having an argument or winning a debate or making a point. It is an attempt to represent God and present His gospel so that people who are without hope might discover the hope you have; and therefore they also will have confidence and conviction in times of trouble. Confidence and conviction go hand in hand and must be cherished and nourished.

A Matter of Conscience

Peter adds, "keeping a clear conscience, so that those who speak maliciously against your good behavior . . . may be ashamed of their slander." This note has been sounded before, so we do not need to sustain it. When we try really hard to stand for the things of God we will meet no little opposition. Many accusations will be made about which we can do nothing. But there is one thing we can and must do: We must maintain a clear conscience.

I vividly remember the testimony of a young missionary. When she was in Bible college she worked in a high-fashion store and over the years she robbed her employer of thousands of dollars worth of goods. One day God got through to her about her gross inconsistency. She went to her classmates, the authorities in the school, and to her employer and made a full confession. She also made a promise to repay the man every penny she had taken from him. She not only did that but, when she was through, she led him to Christ. Her sensational story was hardly normal missionary fare and I was interested in the reaction! Some people thought she should not make such a confession, but she said, "Listen, when you've confessed it, you're forgiven. When you're forgiven there is nothing to hide. When there is nothing to hide there is nothing to fear, and when there is nothing to fear you're free."

The trouble with conscience is that we can starve it so it becomes weak. Or we can do what Paul told Timothy (1 Tim. 4:2), "Sear it with a hot iron," and it will lose all sensitivity. Conscience needs to be in touch all the time with the enlightened truth of God's Word, and then it will be ready, along with confidence and conviction, for whatever tough times may lie ahead.

FIFTEEN

SUFFERING
1 Peter 3:17-22

We know that people suffer because of evil and we are aware that some people suffer for doing good. But Peter strikes a new note when he says, "It is better, if it is God's will, to suffer for doing good than for doing evil." To say, "It is God's will that we suffer" is to introduce a powerful factor in our understanding of the mystery of suffering. People react to suffering in a variety of ways. Some have decided that there cannot possibly be a God because of all the suffering in the world, while others, who may not wish to deny His existence, certainly question His apparent impotence to check it or His amoral acceptance of it. Many who believe there is a God and have had a deep faith in Him have become very angry at God when suffering has come their way. So suffering is a highly volatile subject. Very often attitudes toward suffering are closely related to attitudes towards God which, in turn, affect attitudes to the rest of life.

Insight into the Sufferings of Christ

Christians have a unique approach to suffering. They recognize that they don't understand many aspects of suffering but they do understand that God identified with humanity in our suffering. He sent His only begotten Son to die on the cross where He suffered infinitely more than we have ever suffered. Furthermore, Christians, having chosen to identify with the suffering Christ, know that they cannot expect to be exempt from suffering themselves.

The sufferings of Christ were foreordained. Peter speaks of the prophets' desire to understand what the Spirit meant when He predicted the sufferings of Christ and the glory that was to follow. In other words, the Old Testament predicts that He will be a suffering Messiah. Therefore, Peter concludes that the sufferings of Christ were not accidental; and they were not explicable in terms of sociological concerns, the result of human antagonisms or even a good man suffering because He was surrounded by evil men. The sufferings and death of Christ, foreordained of God, far from being God's plan coming unglued, were God's plan coming to fruition.

Before man was created, God knew exactly that the whole plan He had for the human race was going to be centered in His Son, our Lord, who would save through suffering. Nothing makes this clearer than the brilliant biblical phrase, "The Lamb that was slain from the creation of the world" (Rev. 13:8).

The sufferings of Christ were propitiatory. The expression "Christ died for our sins" is very important because it states that the plan of God has to do with the sins of humanity. We cannot forgive our own sins. Suppose somebody got upset with me and punched me on the nose. While I am recovering from the blow I mumble, "I forgive you"; but unaccountably the attacker says, "You don't need to. I forgave myself." At that point somebody jumps up and says, "Listen, you two, don't argue about it. Neither of you needs to forgive anybody. I forgive you both." A third party couldn't forgive somebody for punching me on the nose, and somebody who punches me on the nose couldn't forgive himself either! Only the punchee can forgive the puncher!

All sin is against God, and some people seem to think they can sin against God and then forgive themselves, while others think that somebody else can forgive them. The Bible puts it in perspective with the question, "Who can forgive sin but God only?" But the big question is "Will He?" And the answer is Yes! He does not overlook sin, for that would be unjust. He gives His Son to take the consequences of sin, thus satisfying divine justice, leaving God perfectly free to forgive sin. So the sufferings of Christ are propitiatory.

The sufferings of Christ are substitutionary. Peter in his effort to clearly explain Christ's suffering adds the expression, "the righteous for the unrighteous" (1 Pet. 3:18). Christ was perfectly righteous before God, so there was no thought of Him being judged for His own sin. He was dying on behalf of those who were not right with God. We understand the substitute rule in sports. If somebody isn't playing very well the coach will pull him off the field and put somebody else in his place. Christ died on the cross for our sins because when it comes down to a matter of forgiveness only He is capable of handling the situation.

The sufferings of Christ are conclusive. "Christ died for sins *once for all*" (v. 18, italics added). In Hebrews 10 we have a number of similar statements such as, "When this priest [that is, Christ] had offered for all time one sacrifice for sins, he sat down at the right hand of God. . . . By one sacrifice he has made perfect forever those who are being made holy" (vv. 12,14). Both the writer to the Hebrews and Peter set the sufferings of Christ in sharp contrast to other religious systems which require ongoing sacrifices. They were thinking of the ancient Jewish sacrificial system, and possibly some of the pagan systems. Even some aspects of contemporary religion promote the idea that sacrifices for sin must continue, but this is a gross misunderstanding. When Christ died for sins He did it once and for all. There is no necessity for any other sacrifice. His death was total satisfaction for all the sins of all people of all time and under all circumstances.

The sufferings of Christ were reconciliatory. This definitive statement further teaches that "Christ died for sins . . . *to bring you to God*" (1 Pet. 3:18, italics added). God made man in the first place in order that man might know Him, love Him, serve Him and enjoy Him forever. But if we ask the average man and average woman, "Do you know God, do you love God, do you enjoy God, do you serve God?" they probably would not understand the question. This clearly indicates the alienation between God and man. Even if it were not clearly shown in human experience, it is unequivocally stated in Scripture, "Your sins have separated between you and your God." Therefore one of the greatest needs in the world is for God and man to be brought back to each other. Attempts to do this from our side of the gulf won't work because we don't have the materials or the inclination to get back to Him. Our only hope then is for God to take the initiative, work from His side to us and have us reconciled to Him. On the cross Christ becomes a bridge across the great gulf between God and man. Through His sufferings He makes it possible for mankind, repentantly, to come through Him, over the gulf into His presence to be warmly welcomed by a reconciling and a forgiving God.

The sufferings of Christ were extraordinary. When Peter wrote, "He was put to death in the body" (v. 18), he used a brutal word which means He was executed. Christ died in the most ignominious way a man could die. All that human ingenuity had been able to invent down through the long, sad history of human perversion had found its ultimate in crucifixion.

Of all the deaths that Christ could have died, that the Father could have foreordained for His sinless Son, crucifixion was the worst. This may be because God was not only wanting to identify with our suffering and our sin, but He was wanting to do it at a depth deeper than any we had ever known, and suffer more than we could ever suffer in order to prove His unspeakable love for us. But this leads us to the next statement which is somewhat difficult to understand. He was executed in the body but "made alive by [or in] the Spirit." The word *Spirit* is capitalized meaning "the Holy Spirit"; but it could just as accurately have a small *s* meaning "the human spirit." Nobody knows conclusively, but I want to suggest that Peter is speaking of the human spirit of Christ in contrast to the body which suffered brutal execution.

Christ's death was terrible but temporary because He was executed in the body and immediately made alive in His spirit; and for three days and nights He moved in the nether regions. We can't be dogmatic about this because we don't know the details, but it would appear that Peter is saying that the Lord Jesus, quickened in spirit, "went and preached to the spirits in prison." Speculations about the identity of these "spirits in prison" abound and dogmatism on the subject may not be in order. Some have used this statement as a basis for believing that after the unconverted die they get another chance to be converted. This idea should not be encouraged for a number of reasons, not least of which is the special word translated *preach*. One Greek word for *preach* means "to proclaim the gospel or to evangelize" while another word means "to declare or to make an announcement." Peter uses the latter and apparently means that Christ went into the regions "under the earth" and made a declaration to the forces of death and darkness that He is greater for He lives in the power of an endless life. Later He was to rise from the dead to the Father's right hand, but already He shows after His apparent defeat that He is Victor. Suffering to be understood by the believer must be viewed through the prism of the sufferings of Christ.

Identification with the Sufferings of Christ

Peter, on one occasion, said that he found some of the things Paul had written rather hard to understand. I'd like to know what Paul thought about the next piece of Peter's work! Peter's thoughts start bouncing off each other like balls on a pool table. They collide with one another and promptly head in new directions. Try to follow his train of thought as he starts talking about our suffering. That triggers his thinking about the suffering of Christ. So he talks about His death but he can't talk about that without thinking of Him being "quickened in spirit." This leads to what He did when He was quickened in spirit as He declared His victory to the spirits. Those spirits were in their present state because of the rebellion round about the time of Noah; so he detours to Noah and talks about the flood. The flood reminds him of water and water suggests baptism which, of course, speaks of Christians identifying with a suffering Christ. Relentless logic if you can follow it!

It is doubtful if there is a better illustration of God's dealings with man than the story of Noah and the flood. God looked down on the earth and was appalled with man's condition, and He said, "I'm sorry I made them" (see Gen. 6:5-7). The moral order of our universe, with which we all agree, requires that wrong should be punished and right should be rewarded. This order originated with God, so the inevitability of judgment follows hard on the heels of the sin of man.

But God also exhibits grace and patience. God's justice must judge sin but His grace reaches out to those who are sinning. He chose to bring a judgment of water but also provided a means of escape so that the water which would destroy some would be the means of saving others. Some would sink under, others would sail over!

Peter says that the story of the flood is an *anti-tupos* of baptism. The Greek word *tupos* described the blow of a hammer hitting metal and producing a clanging sound. The "anti-clang" is, therefore, an "echo." Peter says that the flood is an "echo" of baptism and that baptism is "the pledge" or "answer" of a good conscience towards God. We might ask, "If baptism is the answer, what is the question?" I would suggest it is the question of God to man—"How do you hope to be reconciled to me?" And the answer in dramatic symbolism is, "By identifying with the crucified and risen Son through whom my sins were forgiven!"

Involvement in the Sufferings of Christ

It is reasonable to assume that having identified with the suffering Saviour we might become involved in His sufferings.

Christians must expect to suffer, first of all, *because of antagonism to Christ*. Many people don't like Jesus Christ. They don't like what He represents so they don't like His representatives either. They may get along fine with you if you "keep your mouth shut" and refrain from "stuffing Christianity down their throats"; but once identified with Him there is no way to avoid identifying with many of His unpopular positions and catching some of the antagonism which comes with the positions.

Christians also suffer because they take stands against evil. I'm afraid many Christians have made their name for what they are against rather than what they favor. We must be fundamentally positive, but when we identify with Christ we state we are for what He is for, but also against what He is against. That's when the fur begins to fly! Many people don't mind Christians being religious in a corner, but standing against evil involves stepping on toes!

In Washington recently a "pro-choice" marcher

carried a sign saying, "Keep your nasty morality off my body." She was saying, "I do it my way, you do it your way, but don't try and put your way on me because if you do I'll take you on." Christians have a long tradition of taking a stand against evil, and when they do, somebody suffers and often it is the Christian.

Christians sometimes fall into sin themselves and suffer for their own stupidity. I get upset when I hear the devil being blamed for Christian stupidity. This thinking is as inadequate as that of Flip Wilson, the comedian, who popularized the slogan, "The devil made me do it." The devil can't make us do anything we don't agree to do. The Holy Spirit will empower our will and nerve our faint endeavor, but if we decide to follow temptation, to do what is wrong and contravene God's law, there is no exemption from consequences, and suffering for spiritual stupidity and stubbornness is to be expected.

Christians also suffer because they are part of a fallen world. The whole creation is groaning and creaking, longing for the day when everything will be redeemed and made anew. All kinds of crazy and cruel things are happening and we're not in an airtight capsule in the middle. We're part of it and we'll suffer with it.

Sometimes Christians suffer because it is the will of God that they should. Peter tells us on a number of occasions in this Epistle that suffering is allowed by God to prove that our faith is genuine. One day the devil had a word with the Lord about Job. "What have you been doing?" said the Lord.

"I've been running to and fro having a look at your people."

"What do you think of them?"

"I don't like them!"

"Well, have you considered my servant Job?"

"Oh, Job, he is a faithful man, but look what you have given him. He's got everything! But take it all away and then see if he remains true to you."

God said, "Alright." Calamity fell, Job suffered, and his faith didn't falter! Sometimes God will allow calamity to come to see where our faith lies. Not only did Job display his faith so powerfully, but he also glorified God by his steadfast commitment to Him through utter deprivation and constant encouragement to "curse God and die."

Satan returned to the Board Room of Hell knowing that he was beaten by a pathetic man sitting on a garbage heap, scratching his open sores with pieces of pots but resting his tired body and aching heart in the merciful hands of an ultimately triumphant God. Christians in all ages have had the same opportunity to live for His glory when the going gets tough!

SIXTEEN

TAKING UP THE CROSS
1 Peter 4:1-6

The Lord Jesus told His disciples during their training, "Anyone who dares not take his cross and follow me is not worthy of me" (Matt. 10:38). Modern-day disciples sometimes complain about their arthritis and bravely say, "I suppose it is my cross." Others regard a difficult marriage in the same way and say, "I suppose we all have our cross to bear." We should never confuse arthritis and husbands with crosses. To take up the cross is not to put up with the inevitable and put on a brave face. Jesus Christ took up His cross intelligently, willingly and joyfully because He knew it was the Father's will. To take up the cross is to accept the will of God in the same manner as Christ did, fully recognizing that it will involve some degree of pain and discomfort as it did for Him.

The problem that confronted the disciples was that they knew what it meant in their society to take up the cross, but they had no idea what possible connection there could be between taking up the cross and being worthy of their master. It was common in those days to be executed by crucifixion. And those unfortunate people being so executed were required to carry the cross-beam on their shoulders, bearing an announcement of their name, where they came from and their crimes, through the crowded, narrow streets of Jerusalem. It was a matter of great shame, an experience of terrible trauma. What Jesus meant was beyond the disciples' comprehension because, at that point, He hadn't even told them about His own cross. Peter had come a long way from the time when he first heard Christ's words to the point of writing 1 Peter 4:1-6 in which he gives a full commentary on Jesus' teaching about cross-bearing.

The Appreciation of the Cross as Experienced by Peter

Peter's initial reaction to Christ was favorable. His brother, Andrew, having been introduced to Jesus as "the lamb of God who takes away the sin of the world," promptly went home and told his brother, "We have found the Messiah."

Immediately Simon said to himself, "Great, we need a Messiah around here, a great leader who will restore poor old impoverished Israel to the good old days, back to the golden days of David's kingdom. We need to get these Romans off our backs, to be our own people, to get back to when we were great."

Jesus took one look at Simon and said, "You're Simon but you will be Peter." Peter was intrigued with Jesus and promptly involved himself in what he fully anticipated would be a very exciting escapade. (See John 1:35-42.)

As time went by, however, it became obvious to Peter that Messiah was either losing His nerve or didn't understand His role. He started to get morose and pessimistic. He developed a defeatist attitude. Then one day Jesus announced to His disciples, "When I get up to Jerusalem I'm going to be killed, but on the third day I'll rise again."

Peter became so incensed that he literally stood in front of Jesus and said, "This shall not be." (See Matt. 16:21,22.) Peter was rejecting any concept of the cross. He would not tolerate this kind of talk at all because it had no place in his perception of Messiah's role. In the Garden of Gethsemane it was Peter who grabbed the sword and tried to defend his Master, only to be humiliated again as Jesus healed the ear of Malchus which Peter had enthusiastically chopped off. (See John 18:10; Luke 22:50,51.)

It is not uncommon for people to have their own ideas of Messiah. They know what needs to be done, and, provided they can find somebody who agrees with them, they can manufacture their own Messiah and create their own Christ. All over Christendom there are people who reject flatly any concept of the cross of Christ. They are happy to have a Christ who fits into their preconceptions and a Messiah who organizes things the way they want them to be organized; but they would take their stand with Peter against a Messiah who starts talking about a cross, sin and hell. They welcome a Christ who will come as an additive to their lives and sweeten the pot, making everything good even better, and everything great, absolutely superb. But a Christ who has a cross is totally repugnant to them. Like Peter they won't even let Christ have a cross—let alone take up theirs.

Later on, when it became obvious that the Lord was going to the cross, Peter denied any connection with Him. He defected. But one day the Lord Jesus appeared, cooked breakfast for him and said, "Peter, I want to ask you a simple question. Do you love me?" Now that was a hard question for Peter to answer because Jesus was really asking, "Do you love the Christ that I am as opposed to the Christ you created to suit your own purposes?" At this point Peter began to understand the cross because he began to understand the reality of who Jesus is. His answer was life changing, "Yes, I love you." (See John 21:15-17.) This confession prepared Peter to receive the whole concept of the cross, the whole content of Calvary.

As he embarked on his apostolic ministry, Peter proclaimed the stupendous fact that Jesus was crucified on the cross partly because of the sinfulness of man but basically according to "God's set purpose and foreknowledge" (Acts 2:23). Years later in his pastoral ministry, as exhibited in the Epistles, he wrote, "Christ died for sins once for all, the righteous for the unrighteous, to bring you to God" (1 Pet. 3:18).

Slowly but surely, over the years Peter had come to a solid appreciation of the Cross of Christ. We need to trace the steps of our understanding to ensure that we rightly relate to the Christ of Calvary.

The Application of the Cross as Explained by Peter

The word "therefore" links what is gone with what is coming. It ties principle to practice. Some people love doctrine but are not interested in applying it; other people just want practice, as they can't be bothered with doctrine. The Bible doesn't encourage either position; it outlines principles, inserts a "therefore" and launches into the practical application. Peter having shown how he has come to appreciate the cross now begins to apply the cross in his own life.

Applying the cross to our attitudes. "Therefore, since Christ suffered in his body, arm yourselves also with the same attitude, because he who suffered in his body is done with sin" (1 Pet. 4:1). When Christ went to the cross He assumed our sin, the sin of all people in all situations, under all circumstances, for all ages. He then accepted the wrath of God against our sin and assumed, personally, the penalty of our sin—"Christ died for our sin." Having been utterly sinless He became the personification of sin, the focal point of judgment and in Himself the satisfactory propitiation for our sin. The moment He died He was done with sin.

He had nothing to do with sin before He came into the world; he tolerated a sinful environment and identified with sinful people while He was in the world; on the cross He became sin for us. His experience of sin built up in a remorseless, excruciating crescendo until, with a triumphant cry, He died for sin. At that moment He was through with sin forever.

It ought to be rather obvious that we who claim the merits of His death agree with His attitude towards sin and show it by saying that we wish to be done with it too. That means applying the cross to our attitudes. One of the contemporary attitudes towards sin is to call it by other names. Perhaps the "products of genetic imbalance," the "result of environmental considerations," or "parental abuse." Some call it "an alternative life-style." We've got a plethora of substitute names for sin.

This is not to imply that many of the things going on in our world aren't alternative life-styles. They are choices or alternatives, but they are wrong choices and poor alternatives. Neither do we believe that environments and genetic considerations don't have bearing on our lives. But we must insist that while environment and heredity and family situations all produce certain inclinations and propensities towards sin, sinners decide to sin in the end. There may be all kinds of forces, all kinds of opportunities, all kinds of circumstances—but none of them can make us sin. In the final analysis, sin is a choice.

One of the first things we do, therefore, is to start calling sin, sin. Then we encourage sinners to apply the cross to their attitude toward sin by developing a new attitude which, instead of excusing and condoning sin, will say it is incompatible with Christian conviction; therefore, choose to be through with it. There is much more to dealing with sin, but this is what Peter explains at this point.

Recently a young pastor told me, "For many years I have been working as a social worker involving myself in many difficult situations, but I was limited in what I could say and do. Now that I am a pastor I can open the Scriptures, apply biblical principles, sit down with people, and help them work through their problems, including facing their sin. In a few months in the pastorate I've seen more lives changed than in many years as a social worker." That's not a put-down of social work, but we accept that at the root of most of our problems are fundamentally sinful, selfish choices, and that the only antidote to those choices is a cross on our attitudes.

Applying the cross to our ambitions. Peter continues, "As a result, he does not live the rest of his earthly life for evil human desires, but rather for the will of God" (v. 2). Peter talks about "the rest of [your] earthly life" with particular reference to your ambitions for the rest of your earthly life. It is quite possible that our ambitions for the rest of life are fundamentally selfish. That being the case, we will fit comfortably into our society because that's just about what everybody is feeling about ambitions—to be comfortable, to be popular, to make a profit, to be exempt from pain and to be guaranteed pleasure. These ambitions are all rooted in "me" and "mine" and "my." The problem with these human desires is that they can easily rule God out and then they become sinful.

There is an alternative position which is to say something like, "Lord, I fully realize that you have a plan for my life but my plan and your plan are in tension. My ambition, if I am perfectly honest, is to do what I want to do, and I would love your endorsement on my choices despite the fact that they are contrary to your choices; but I know it cannot work so I must apply a cross to my ambitions. And I remember that a cross is an 'I' ruled out."

The cross was not primarily intended as an 18-carat gold ornament, or as a Christian symbol in religious places. It was intended for dying on, dying, among other things, to that determination to go my own way, and coming to the position, "Not my will, but thine be done." This doesn't mean that we cease to be ambitious, but rather we are ambitious for what God wants.

I talked with a delightful couple recently—sharp young people, well trained. He has a master's in education; she is an English teacher. They were very happy. Everything in life was coming together for them and then it suddenly dawned on them that perhaps they ought to explore what God wanted to do with their lives. They arrived at a startling conclusion. Of all things, God wants them to teach English! What's startling about that? He wants them to teach English in Chung King, China. So they are in the process of packing their bags, getting their visas, going behind the bamboo curtain, seeking to be a presence for Christ in that new environment. Ambitious for one thing only—the will of God. The will of God does not mean we have to go to China, but it does mean a cross to personal ambition and a crown on God's design.

Applying the cross to our activities. Peter's description of the pagan life is graphic and his rejection of it is unequivocal. "You have spent enough time in the past doing what the pagans choose to do—living in debauchery, lust, drunkenness, orgies, carousing and detestable idolatry" (v. 3). Pagan life involved all kinds of iniquity, impurity, and idolatry. The word "detestable" means that which even the Roman Empire wouldn't tolerate.

The Christians to whom Peter writes were not fourth- and fifth-generation Christians who were getting increasingly bored with each generation. They were fresh, newly-converted pagans. They had all been up to their necks in pagan life-style which had picked up such momentum that it was carrying over to their Christian activities. They were prone to accept what even Rome declared unacceptable! Peter calls them to put a cross on these activities which are relics of the old life and contradictions to the new. The key, of course, is the phrase "doing what pagans choose to do." If pagans can choose to do things, converted pagans can choose *not* to do them. This is applying the cross.

Not only terribly bad things have to be dealt with either. In my life some very good and beautiful things have had a cross put on them too. Many years ago when I was in my early twenties I sang in a championship choir in Kendal, England. We practiced Tuesday nights—the only night I had free. At that time I was studying and preaching and working, so the Greenside Choir was my relaxation and hobby, and I loved it. I began to feel decidedly uneasy about it and one day I got the feeling that I ought to resign. I went to the director of the choir, explained, and she said, "Just tell me why, Stuart, why?"

I said, "I'm terribly sorry, I can't. It has something to do with a Christian conviction that even I do not understand. You just have to believe me, this is no reflection on you." So I resigned, reluctantly, but knowing that in some way God was saying, "Put a cross on that activity."

The following day somebody asked me, "Stuart, what do you do on Tuesday nights?"

I replied, "I resigned from the Greenside Choir last night so my Tuesdays are free—it's the only night of the week that is free."

He said, "Good. A group of us have been praying that you would come to our town each Tuesday and teach the Bible to a small group of earnest people." About the third week of the study an elderly lady became a believer. A week or two later she died and I've often thought about the cross on my choir. Sometimes it comes down hard on the beautiful as well as the unthinkable.

Applying the cross to our associations. Peter appears to speak from personal experience as he adds, "They think it strange that you do not plunge with them into the same flood of dissipation, and they heap abuse on you" (v. 4). The people we used to associate with in all kinds of actions that were contrary to Christ understandably get very upset with us if we pull out. They don't mind us being Christians as long as we continue in "the flood of dissipation." In fact, they will be most tolerant. They say things like, "That's neat! That's great! We're glad for you. You're into Jesus—we're into jogging. This salvation bit makes you feel good; we feel better because we're on a diet with plenty of roughage! Different strokes, different folks." But when we find it necessary to say, "I'm sorry, deal me out; I'm sorry, I'm through; this is wrong for me now," things can change dramatically. The tolerance and bonhomie dissipate into thin air, and, as Peter says, they begin to heap abuse on you.

I'm not advocating evangelical isolation, but there has to be a very clear-cut differentiation in the Christian's life between his Christianity and his involvement in ambitions, attitudes, activities and associations which, in themselves, are contrary to Christ. Christ died for sin and is done with it—we died in Him, and we're done with it too. The cross has been applied and this is not once and for all; it's an ongoing experience.

The Appeal of the Cross as Expressed by Peter

Those who heap abuse on believers "will have to

give account to him who is ready to judge the living and the dead" (v. 5). Everybody is going to appear in the court of the judge. The One who will sit in the court as our Judge is the One who hung on the cross as our Jesus. There will be four categories of people standing before the judge to give an account of their lives. There are those who will be alive when Christ calls for the great final judgment, and those who will already be dead. Peter calls them "the living and the dead." The living and the dead are then divided into two categories. Some who will be alive when He comes will also be spiritually alive; others will be spiritually dead. Some will be already dead but alive in Christ and some will be both physically dead and spiritually dead on the judgment day. There will be (1) living living and (2) dead living, (3) living dead and (4) dead dead at the judgment.

This is what will happen. The Judge will bring everything into account. The living and the dead who are alive in Christ because they appreciated the cross and applied it to their lives, were forgiven and became disciples will be told to enter into the joy of the Lord. The living and dead who are dead to Christ because they rejected the cross, manufactured their own messiah, created their own Christ and have absolutely no antidote for their sin will be told by Judge Jesus, "Depart from me. I never knew you."

The cross is the central factor in the coming judgment and disciples who recognize its majestic significance also demonstrate their understanding of its ongoing relevance by taking up their cross daily and following Christ.

SEVENTEEN

LIVING NEAR THE END
1 Peter 4:7-11

"The end of all things is near," said the Apostle Peter as he contemplated Nero's bizarre behavior, the persecution looming on the horizon and the probability that he himself would not survive much longer. As he looked at his particular circumstances he had a tremendous sense that time was limited. But there was more than that in his mind.

Christian Belief Concerning "The End"

There is a fundamental principle in Scripture which, simply stated, says, "In the beginning God created the heavens and the earth and in the end God will destroy the heavens and the earth." As surely as God, through His creative word, brought into existence the things that exist, so God, through His irrefutable command, will terminate all the things that He brought into being. God, the initiator and the sustainer of all things, also is the terminator of all things. The Bible teaches an end to human history brought about by divine intervention.

Peter, as a Jew, had been taught from the Old Testament about something called "the day of the Lord." The people of Israel quite rightly believed that they were God's chosen people. They recognized that they had failed Him on many occasions, and had suffered much through their captivities. But even in the darkest hour God, through His prophets, always had a message of hope for them. It was a hope that one day Israel would be what she was intended to be. The day of the Lord would come!

Israel also believed that the surrounding nations were the heathen. They believed that the heathen quite rightly deserved the judgment of God. The "day of the Lord," as the Jewish people understood it in Old Testament times, therefore would be the day of Israel's vindication; the day of the nations' judgment. They saw it as a great cataclysmic event.

Peter thoroughly believed this as did the other disciples of our Lord Jesus. They were not able, therefore, to appreciate the heartbeat of the Master as they saw Him grieving over Jerusalem, and saying, "Oh, Jerusalem, Jerusalem . . . your house is left to you desolate" (Luke 13:34,35). But His disciples obviously didn't want to listen as He predicted awful things for Jerusalem. They were too excited to be in the big city. They came from Galilee and were rather like kids from the country in New York for the first time, staring at the Empire State Building. As they excitedly shouted, "Look at these buildings! We don't have anything like that in Galilee," the Lord Jesus said, "There won't be one stone left standing on another in this city."

The disciples were puzzled and later came to Him quietly and said, "Master, Master, tell us when will this happen to Jerusalem, and when will be the time of your coming and when will be the end of the age?" (see Mark 13:1-4). Now notice they asked three intertwined questions which show that the disciples understood that "the day of the Lord" would incorporate the coming of Christ in glory.

They also assumed that if Jerusalem was going to be destroyed it would be when God would terminate all things, because, as far as they were concerned, if Jerusalem was destroyed that was the end of everything. The Lord Jesus did not unravel these three ideas but He did show them that there will be a climactic, cataclysmic intervention of God in human affairs which will terminate history, and that this will take place at the glorious appearing and revelation of His Son, our Lord Jesus Christ. The only question remaining in the minds of the disciples related to the timing of it.

As Peter stood up to preach on the day of Pentecost he explained that the "end times" were beginning—that at that particular moment of history the last days were dawning! How long the last days will last, however, remains a mystery locked up in the mind of God. Furthermore, Peter in his second Epistle gives more details about the end of the world. He tells us that the heavens and the earth will dissolve with fervent heat under God's direction. The same God who made all things is reserving these things for judgment and He, having initiated, will then terminate all things.

Everybody knows perfectly well that the overriding concern of the statesmen of our day and age is whether we can handle the tremendous nuclear resources stockpiled in the arsenals of the super-powers. Some leaders feel that the only way to handle it is to maintain detente with Russia. So far it has worked. To prove it, we're still here! Others have decided a more aggressive approach is called for. It remains to be seen if they are right; but, of course, if they are wrong, we won't be here to know it! This is the situation in which we find ourselves at the present time, 19 hundred years after Peter's powerful phrase, "The end of all things is near." The only thing is we don't know how near.

There is another aspect which we must not overlook. None of us knows how near our end is in the sense of the termination of our individual lives. One day in Hong Kong I forgot, momentarily, that the traffic travels on the left side of the road. I stepped in front of a vehicle going at a tremendous speed and I'll guarantee it didn't miss me by more than an inch. Suddenly it dawned on me that I had been less than an inch from eternity. In this sense the end is so near; it is never more than one breath away.

Now, of course, this kind of topic can get people paranoid in a hurry. But Peter is not interested in producing paranoia, but in producing living that is consistent with "the end."

Christian Behavior Considering "The End"

Peter gives a list of seven things that should characterize "end time" living.

First, keep a cool head. "Be clear minded and self-controlled" may sound strange coming from the pen of one who has just announced that the end is imminent. But Peter insists that Christians don't panic—they pray; and to pray properly they must hold things together between their ears.

Now how do we pray in panic situations? The best person to answer that is Peter himself. The Lord Jesus had told the disciples to be witnesses unto Him—the authorities forbade them to do it. They went ahead anyway, were thrown in jail, threatened, beaten and let go. They promptly went back to their church fellowship. When they got back they said, "Don't panic; let's pray." How they prayed is recorded in Acts 4. They started off their prayer with the words, "Sovereign Lord." In panic situations start off by reminding yourself who is in control: the "Sovereign Lord, maker of heaven and earth and the sea and all that is under them." Now that's a good reminder that the Sovereign Lord, having made all things, is not going to let anybody else destroy His creation—He is going to do it!

Then they quoted the Bible, Psalm 2 to be precise. A cool head is necessary to remember what the Bible says and to apply what it says to the immediate situation. If we panic in difficult situations there is a very real possibility that we'll pray a lot of garbage which will only exacerbate the problem. Having cleared the ground by basing everything on God's Word and sovereignty, they prayed "Lord, give thy servants boldness so that they may witness effectively." Their prayer was not for survival, but revival. This really requires a cool head because panicky people usually tend to pray panicky prayers for personal protection.

Second, keep a steady balance. It's very easy to become unbalanced when we think of the end times. When Peter talked about the end of all time, many said, "Oh come on. You don't really believe that, do you? Everything continues the way it has from the very beginning." Now people talk like that today. They say, "We've got problems, I'll admit, but we'll solve them. I mean things are difficult, no question about it, but we'll handle it."

One of the most eminent men in Wisconsin has a firm conviction that education holds the solution for everything. I've talked to him, I like him, but I don't buy his philosophy that education will solve everything! Neither education nor any other human effort will solve the problem we've got when God decides, "Enough is enough." We can't handle that one, folks, so we must not stick our heads in the sand and hope it will go away. It won't—the end is near.

Other folks become so excited about the whole concept they decide to drop out of school. They have tried every other excuse, but this is the biggie! No one could knock this. The Lord is coming again. Some people try to say God has called them to the ministry but they don't want to go to seminary or Bible school because the Lord is coming again. Some people decide that they won't equip themselves for a career because the Lord is coming again. Every generation of Christians has believed that they lived in the last of the last days, and they were all wrong! So by the law of averages there is a good chance those who go overboard in their approach to living in the end times will need to be rescued from drowning in their enthusiasm by those whose approach was more balanced.

An astronaut bound for the moon was asked, "How will you get off the moon?"

He said, "We fire the rockets and we take off in our little module."

"But what happens if it doesn't fire?"

He said, "Then we're stuck."

"How long will your life-support system last?"

"Six hours."

The reporter then asked, "May I ask you what you will do for the last six hours?"

"Sure," he said. "I'll work on the engine!"

When we believe the coming of the Lord is near, we continue what we were doing for the simple reason we have gotten into the habit of doing what He told us to do. Just maintain the balance of expectancy and anticipation that we will live our full lives and die before He comes, but if He comes first that will be just fine! The believer in tune with Him simply keeps on fixing the engine!

Third, keep a warm heart. "Above all, love each other deeply, because love covers over a multitude of sins" (4:8) is the next piece of instruction. The words "above all" mean that love is the supreme Christian virtue.

When I joined the marines I was given a high pile of equipment which I had no idea how to use. An instructor saw me under the pile and said, "Don't worry about all that. Just learn how to fit your belt on; everything else fits on it. If your belt is not right, nothing is right." Christians who worry about all their spiritual equipment might find it helpful to make sure their belt—in this case, love—fits properly, then other things will fit too.

The word translated "deeply" describes a sprinter or a race horse stretching for the finish line. We are to stretch ourselves to love, to recognize the supremacy of love and to keep a warm heart.

I heard a story about an Englishman who came over to work at one of the rubber plants in Akron. His first Sunday in town he went to the pastor and said, "I'm here for two years, I'm British, I'm a Christian and I want to serve in this church.

Please put me to work!" The pastor introduced him to a few people and he quickly became one of the best-known people in the fellowship. There was never a Sunday when he didn't eat lunch with a different family in the church, not because he invited himself but because they all wanted to know him. He believed what the Bible says, "If any man would have friends he must first show himself friendly!" If we wait for somebody to love us we'll find they are waiting too. So we must start stretching and start reaching out because the end is near.

Fourth, keep an open house. "Offer hospitality to one another without grumbling" (v. 9). The word for *hospitality* is literally the "love of strangers" or "the love of foreigners." The word *xenophobia*, "the fear of strangers" has found a place in our vocabulary but *philoxenia*, "the love of strangers," needs to appear in Christian terminology. In the New Testament days hospitality without grumbling was particularly important. The church in those days didn't have a sanctuary, a Christian education wing, gyms, administration blocks or mortgages! They met in homes because that was all they had.

When the fellowship met on Sunday mornings that meant somebody had to be given to hospitality, preferably without grumbling because a sour face can work most effectively on a worship service. Not only that, traveling evangelists did not stay at the Hilton. They had a choice between Christian homes and flea-ridden dens of iniquity. In actual fact, the life and growth of the church was measurable in terms of the hospitable spirit of those early Christians.

In addition, when people were thrown out of

their homes and ostracized by their families because they become Christians, they could not live on the streets. Christian homes took them in. They took in freed slaves and women who had been left by their husbands. Hospitality was the stuff of which the early church was made.

One of the great delights of Christian living is to use our homes instead of just preserving them for ourselves. If they can be used for a weekly study or for the kids to come into, that's great. Perhaps, more realistically, we should consider a special hospitality problem in our day. Somebody who is deeply concerned about the abortion issue told me he was so glad that evangelicals are speaking out on the abortion issue, but he added a word of warning: "Before you shout too much about stopping abortions, have you made provision for the little gals who are pregnant out of wedlock? If you're saying 'don't abort,' what are you saying to the girl whose mother and father has kicked her out and her boyfriend has split for the Sun Belt? What are you going to do with that little gal?" Then he said, "If you are not prepared to open your home and take that girl in for nine months maybe you should mute your criticism of abortion!" Be given to hospitality!

Fifth, keep a faithful attitude. "Each one should use whatever gift he has received to serve others, faithfully administering God's grace in its various forms" (v. 10). We know about God's grace. He graciously saves those who don't deserve it. We know about His grace which gives different gifts to those He has saved. We also know that He gives these gifts that they might be used for the benefit of all. So we are trustees on the understanding that on the Day of the Lord He will evaluate what we did with that which He entrusted to us. His sole concern on that day will be "did we live faithfully?" As we consider the end of our days we should ask ourselves one question, "Will He say to me, 'Well done, good and faithful servant'?"

Sixth, keep a pure message. There is a special privilege in hearing God's Word and a peculiar pleasure in doing God's will, but we must never overlook the particular pressure to share the Word of God. Handled properly the Word produces fruit abundantly in the lives of the receptors, so Peter's admonition, "If anyone speaks, he should do it as one speaking the very words of God" (v. 11), is especially significant.

Seventh, keep a powerful witness. Christians following the servant example of the Master need constant reminders of the necessity of nurturing a servant spirit. When reminded that a servant uses "the strength God provides" so that "God may be praised," there is motivation enough. But when seen in the light of the end of all things, any other attitude would appear obscene.

EIGHTEEN
HANDLING HARSH REALITIES
1 Peter 4:12-19

Society seems to suggest that we should always be happy, comfortable and successful. But it ain't necessarily so! This idea is related more to fantasy than reality, and we show our maturity not by indulging in fantasy but by handling reality. This is basically Peter's theme.

The Word of God is sometimes almost brutal in its realism. It talks about the things that matter and it addresses life as it really is. Let us approach this passage in order to ensure that we are in touch with reality as expressed by Scripture.

There is nothing strange about fiery trials. We live in a world that is far from ideal. Everybody can list dozens of things that are wrong with this world. Many people are getting hurt; a lot of people are experiencing difficult times. In a fallen world people do wrong things so people suffer wrong things; we must face the fact that in a sinful, fallen, less-than-ideal world all kinds of painful things will happen.

We also need to notice that God permits these things to happen. As we saw earlier we may suffer "if it is God's will" (3:17). God has graciously determined that His people should not be wafted off to heaven on a pink-edged cloud to sprout wings, polish halos and play harps. He ordained that His people should stay on earth and live realistically in the real world. And what is this real world? It is a world that has many glorious and beautiful aspects, but it is riddled with desperately painful aspects as well.

I was reminded of this recently in Rio de Janeiro. Rio, one of my favorite places on the whole face of God's earth, is indescribably beautiful unless you start looking at the realities of it. Behind one luxury tourist hotel there is a very steep mountainside split by a deep ravine. In this and similar ravines live a hundred thousand people in filthy, crime-infested poverty. The real Rio is not only Sugar Loaf Mountain at sunset and Copacabana on a warm fresh morning but also the homeless orphans and the rickety shanty towns on the steep hillsides. It is in this world of gross inequity and evil imbalance beset by pain and pleasure that God ordained His people should live.

There is nothing strange about having a tough time, as Peter says, and mature believers learn to profit from these things. The immature person is much more likely to react and resent the things that are happening to them even though similar things are happening in the whole of society. So we must not think it is strange when we encounter fiery trials. They are some of the harsh realities of life, permitted by God, from which we can grow.

There is nothing sentimental about the sufferings of Christ. Peter says, "Rejoice that you participate in the sufferings of Christ, so that you may be overjoyed when his glory is revealed" (4:13). Way back before human history it was determined by the Trinity that the Son should participate in this world's sufferings: He was born in poverty; as a child He was a refugee; He had to work very hard; He lived under a repressive political regime; His contemporaries misunderstood Him. In the end He suffered the ignominy of being charged and found guilty when He was innocent. Christ chose to identify with a suffering world, not in a technical sense, but in an intensely practical way. There was nothing sweet and sentimental about His suffering and we should avoid all temptation to rob His sacrificial life-style and death of the harshness and the pain. If we fail to do this we might give ourselves a rationale for fantasy living because we have translated Christ's reality into the fantasy world.

There is nothing surprising about being insulted. Christians sometimes are insulted because of their Christian stance. Now we shouldn't be surprised at this, but some believers are hurt about it. Peter's perspective is important—"If you are insulted because of the name of Christ, you are blessed" (v. 14). Everybody gets hurt when they are insulted, but Christians should learn to be blessed when they are insulted because they are Christians. Let me explain why.

Christ is an insult to man's pride. Man thinks he is alright, or at least not all bad! He knows he isn't perfect but fondly imagines he's pretty close, and with a little attention he can make things satisfactory. But Christ is the anointed Messiah come to do for us what we can't do for ourselves. This concept is an insult to the average person, a blow to his self-sufficiency. When Christ stretches out His arms and says, "I'll do it for you," the person who thinks he can solve everything is insulted by Christ and he reacts by insulting the name of Christ. So we must never be surprised when people insult the name of Christ and we get some of the backwash.

There is nothing spiritual about suffering for wrongdoing. Peter says, "If you suffer, it should not be as a murderer or thief or any other kind of [wrongdoer], or even as a meddler." Christians are rather superb at doing stupid things and then spiritualizing them and getting great glory out of them. Peter sticks a pin in this balloon immediately. If we engage in some illegal activity there will be legal consequences; if we engage in immorality there will be moral consequences; and if we engage in improper activities we may well produce societal displeasure. The Greek word (*allotriepiskopos*) translated "meddler" is as long as it is uncommon. The first half has to do with other people's business. The second means to watch over. If you put it all together it means to watch over other people's affairs or to stick your nose into other people's business!

Christians have a problem at this point. They live in a pluralistic society. Some well-meaning Christians feel responsible for their society. For example, they watch the situation comedies that rarely, if ever, portray what Christians would regard as normal, healthy situations. There is no doubt that some of it does portray a major segment of American society; but Christians feel either that their values should be given at least equal time, or that only Christian values are acceptable. Some have decided that they are going

to take up the fight. They are monitoring pro-
grams, threatening advertisers with boycotts and
generally rattling the networks' cages! Whether
this is the right approach is hotly debated, but
what Peter says is relevant and nondebatable. If we
stick our noses in somebody's business there is a
good chance somebody will whop it! If they do,
don't get all spiritual about it because a simple law
of life states that he who sticketh in his nose find-
eth a fist on the end of it. Therefore we must check
at all times to see if our activities are illegal,
immoral or are perceived as improper. If they are,
we must not spiritualize the tough circumstances
that result.

*There is nothing shameful about being a
Christian.* "However, if you suffer as a Christian,
do not be ashamed, but praise God that you bear
that name" (v. 16). It is interesting to note that the
word *Christian* occurs only three times in the
Scriptures, and Peter is responsible for one usage
in this passage. The word *Christian* has been
totally devalued in our common parlance. The people of Antioch were notorious for giving everybody
nicknames, so they called the people who followed
Christ "Christians," and the Christians accepted
the term even though it was something of an
insult. However, before they accepted the new
name they were known simply as disciples of
Christ.

Christianity stands or falls on Christ. If Christ
is not who He said He is, if Christ didn't do what
He said He did, Christianity is a big hoax. If, on
the other hand, Christ is who He said He is then
Christianity is the only way to go and Christians
have been smart enough to recognize it! To be
Christian doesn't mean to be part of a certain cul-

ture or have a certain morality. To be Christian, fundamentally, is to identify with Christ as Lord and Saviour because of intellectual conviction and moral courage to take the conviction to its necessary conclusion. When that happens we must be ready to defend our position. This is relatively easy because we take our stand on who He is and show that, on the basis of that conviction, there is no real alternative but to be Christian, and if that is the case we don't need to be ashamed.

There are many shameful things about Christians. We're like everybody else—we're sometimes not very nice people. Church history is replete with skeleton-filled cupboards. There are terrible things going on in the name of Christianity at the present time. Northern Ireland is a disaster and much of the hostility is in the name of Christianity. Beirut, in Lebanon, is one of the most beautiful places I've ever seen, but it has been blown to pieces in fearful fighting that includes "Christian militia"! We can't defend some of these things because they are indefensible. We must hang our heads in shame, but never concerning Jesus Christ because we believe He is who He said He is, so we hold our heads high.

There is nothing sacrosanct about the "family" of God. Some people have the idea that when we become Christians we are placed in an airtight bubble and live in a state of spiritual weightlessness, removed and remote from all unpleasantness. But the tough, harsh reality is that judgment will begin with the family of God!

There is going to be judgment. We know, fundamentally, right must be rewarded and wrong must be punished. The surprising thing is that the judgment of God will begin with His people.

Far from being in a position where realities hit everybody else and we escape, Christians can expect to be particularly vulnerable. What this means is that if the family of God doesn't do its job, God will not tolerate it, and church history proves this is true.

In the early days of Christianity the focal point was the Middle East. Today there are lots of beautiful ruins, but you'll look long and hard for the Christian church. The focal point moved from the Middle East to North Africa. Go along the length and breadth of North Africa today; look for the Christian church and you'll find Muslims. Western Europe became the focal point; you'll find Western Europe today is full of superlative, beautiful, gorgeous cathedrals full of emptiness and tourists. From Europe the center of activity moved to North America and there are those who say that already the momentum has moved from North America. Why? Because Christ has shown that if His own people will not accept responsibility and do not face up to accountability, if they think they are exempt from all difficulty, they are not living in reality. We are not sacrosanct, and the harsh reality is that judgment may come sooner than we think.

There is nothing soft about God's will. The Bible does say that God's will is good and perfect and acceptable but it also says, "Those who suffer according to God's will should commit themselves to their faithful Creator" (v. 19). So goodness and acceptability must not be regarded as the same as pleasant and enjoyable. Medicine is good, therapy can be perfect, and surgery acceptable; but none are painless and pleasant.

A pro-golfer friend of mine was doing so well

that he was asked to go to the White House to speak of his success and show how it was related to his faith in Christ. Not long afterwards his game fell apart and he and his family suffered through hard times. When I asked him how he was getting along, he said, "This last year has been a total professional disaster but the most valuable year of my life because I have learned how to grow up."

Some of us need to face up to the fact that we may suffer according to God's will in order that we may be refined like gold in the fire. That hurts! God's will is not soft after all!

It's one thing to know all this but another to know how to handle the situation. Peter says, "Rejoice that you participate in the sufferings of Christ" (v. 13) and "do not be ashamed, but praise God" (v. 16). The first instruction is *be cheerful*. Now be careful about this. It is relatively simple to have a high old time when everything is going well. Some people go to church on Sunday night and let their hair down just a little. They don't have the organ, just drums and guitars! No reformation-era hymn, but something contemporary! Everybody livens up, they clap their hands and they jig around and call it praise. But what happens when the situation changes and the people return to lonely rooms?

Real praise and rejoicing come from deep within the heart, irrespective of the environment, and can be expressed alone in the room or together in the congregation. It wells from the hearts of people who, confronting harsh realities, know what's going on and stand tall in their assurance.

The second instruction is *be content*. Peter

says "you are blessed" (v. 14) if you are insulted for Christ. The word *blessed* is a technical, theological word which really means "filled full" and "content." We don't have too many contented people around. There are many "if onlys" and lots of "why mes," but people who are content are rare. Some people are more docile and amenable than others but this contentment comes because "the Spirit of glory and of God rests on you" (v. 14). It is the power of the Spirit of God that will enable us to stand firm and make us adequate; so He is the source of contentment.

The third instruction is *be considerate*. When talking about judgment and the Christian, Peter shows great sensitivity when he says, "If it begins with us, what will the outcome be for those who do not obey the gospel of God?" (v. 17). One of the unpleasant things about Christians is that we have such a nice time together that we can settle in glorious isolation and let the world go by. But the person who confronts the harsh reality of judgment is driven to compassionate action, to careful living, with the concerns of others deeply etched on the conscience.

The fourth instruction is *be committed*. "So, then, those who suffer according to God's will should commit themselves to their faithful Creator" (v. 19). Our Lord, on the cross, used the same word, "Into your hands I commit my spirit" (Luke 23:46). As we live in a world that is less than ideal He will tell you what to do; the model of our dying Lord's commitment to His Father must always remind us to commit to our faithful Creator.

The final instruction is *be consistent*. Harsh realities produce hard attitudes and unhealthy reactions. But for the Christian the call to "do good" (v. 19) is paramount and will, when obeyed, counteract all other natural reactions.

Harsh realities are here to stay; healthy Christians know that and live healthy lives in the midst of them.

NINETEEN
TAKE ME TO YOUR LEADERS
1 Peter 5:1-4

Christians do not live their Christianity on their own. Having identified with the Lord Jesus they become related to others who are identified with Him. This aspect of spiritual experience is of special significance during times of strain and stress because it enables believers to meet stress in a supportive group situation. It is also important that the group should have good leadership so that both the body and the individuals might handle stress properly.

Peter has a lot to say concerning the church and the leaders of the church (or elders). As a totally committed fisherman it must have frustrated Peter to be required to teach about sheep, flocks and shepherds; but it is a fact that the Bible repeatedly used these familiar expressions to describe people, the church and the leaders.

The People Are Like Sheep
Of all the animals the Lord could have chosen

to describe people, he chose sheep. He could have said we were as brave as lions, as noble as horses, as beautiful as gazelles, but He didn't. This analogy is a singularly unflattering reference to our natural characteristics because, as mentioned previously, sheep are well known for their weakness and their waywardness. The Lord Jesus pointed out that sheep are particularly vulnerable when wild beasts come their way. Many of us have little difficulty seeing that *sheep* is a valid expression describing our weakness because we have been ripped to shreds and we often feel like sheep in the midst of wolves.

The Lord also talked about unscrupulous shepherds who were not interested in the well-being of the sheep but were using the sheep rather than serving them. All of us can pinpoint situations where this has been our unhappy lot. Unfortunately, we have to admit that we are highly susceptible to the wild beasts and unscrupulous shepherds with which our society abounds.

Sheep have a terrible tendency to behave in most unrealistic and unhealthy ways. They love to wander, they have a nose for trouble, and they follow without thinking. There is a natural tendency in our society for people to do things for no other reason than that everybody is doing it.

We have already noted that Peter said, "You were like sheep going astray, but now you have returned to the Shepherd and Overseer of your souls" (1 Pet. 2:25)—a clear echo of Isaiah 53: "We, all like sheep, have gone astray." Peter saw it firsthand as he traveled with the Master. On one occasion the Lord took His disciples for some relaxation time. To their intense frustration, a whole crowd of people came along. The Lord seemed to be concerned for them, but the disciples wanted to get rid of them. The word used to describe Christ's attitude was "that His stomach was tied in knots" and His concern came from His observation that they were "like sheep without a shepherd" (see Mark 6:31-34).

But Peter needed only to turn to his own experience for illustration! When the Lord Jesus quoted Zechariah to His disciples to the effect that God was going to strike the shepherd and the sheep would be scattered, He applied it to His impending death and the resulting flight of the disciples. Peter's response was predictable, "The rest of them may forsake you, but I will never forsake you. I would rather die for you" (see Matt. 26:31-35). When the Lord insisted, Peter would not accept it; so when Peter talks about wayward sheep he's talking very personally because he knows the propensity of his own heart and the weak and wayward tendencies of his fellow sheep.

The Church Is Like a Flock
There is good news for all sheep because the Scriptures teach that if the people are like sheep, the church is like the flock. The Lord Jesus in His well-known passage in John 10 said, "I am the good shepherd; I know my sheep and my sheep know me . . . and there shall be one flock and one shepherd" (vv. 14,16). The intent of our Lord is to gather together out of every kindred and tongue and tribe and nation, from every social and economic and cultural background, people who will acknowledge Him as Shepherd and, therefore, will become one flock.

The Lord was often criticized because of His contact with some rather unsavory characters. His answer, in the form of a parable, was powerful and challenging. "If you were a shepherd and had 100 sheep and lost one you'd leave the 99 and go out and seek the lost one. On finding it you'd put it on your shoulders, bring it back and say, 'Rejoice with me, for I have found my sheep which was lost.' " Exactly the same way, "There is joy in the presence of the angels of heaven over sinners coming to repentance" (see Luke 15:3-7). His uncompromising response to the critics was that shepherds go after wayward, weak sheep to bring them into the community where the shepherd can care for them.

So what is the church? It is a community of wayward, weak individuals who, like sheep, have gone astray. They know that the Good Shepherd gave His life for them, rose again and went after them personally, drawing them to Himself. In repentance they came to Him, committed themselves to Him and became members of the flock of God, just like the fearful group of disciples who were told right from the beginning, "Fear not, little flock."

Hebrews 13 contains a wonderful benediction, "May the God of peace, who through the blood of the eternal covenant brought back from the dead our Lord Jesus, that great Shepherd of the sheep, equip you with everything good for doing his will, and may he work in us what is pleasing to him, through Jesus Christ, to whom be glory for ever and ever, Amen" (vv. 20,21).

Presiding over the flock of redeemed, repentant, wayward, weak sheep is the Great Shepherd who is risen from the dead. His objective is to empower weak, wayward sheep so that they may be equipped to do the work of God as He works in them. The ministry of our Lord Jesus is initially to bring individuals to Himself. Having brought them to Himself, He places them into a massive corporate whole, the church, the body in which the sheer might of His resurrection will be demonstrated as the church becomes a mighty, dynamic force for God in society. That this happened in the early days of the church can be seen in the way the original "little flock" became a mighty army, sweeping across the known world with the transforming message of the Shepherd.

The Bible presents the church as an invisible, universal and mystical body to which all "found" sheep belong. Equally clearly, it speaks of the body as being a local, tangible, visible group of people in a specific geographical location. This group is to be seen as God's special flock in which the Chief Shepherd is empowering the weak and wayward for works of service to the glory of God—a view not always appreciated by those who constitute a local assembly of believers.

These truths need to be strongly emphasized at the present time because it is not uncommon to find people who want to have a Shepherd but don't want anything to do with the flock. (Whoever heard of a Shepherd who doesn't have a flock?) Or worse, they want to be part of a flock that is not interested in a Shepherd who works in the midst of the weak and wayward.

The Elders Are Like Shepherds

When Peter wrote about "elders" his readers were familiar with the expression and the idea. No doubt the Jews among them were aware of what had happened to Moses. He had led a massive crowd of people into the wilderness and he was understandably tired of them. So Moses called together 70 elders and God assured him that the same spirit which rested on Moses rested on every one of them. Multiple eldership was in operation—a principle of operation without which the people of Israel could not have functioned in this tumultuous wilderness experience.

Peter's readers who came from a Gentile background influenced by Rome were no less familiar with elders! The Roman senate was comprised of people who were called the *Senex*—a word meaning "old man." Incidentally, this is the word from which we get "senile" or "senator," and we will make no further comment!

In Jerusalem the Sanhedrin was also called the council of Elders. Peter, as we know, had his own special recollections of dealings with this body of august gentlemen, and the synagogues—which were established as a result of the dispersion of the Jews who had lost their Temple—were directed by elders!

In the light of prevailing principles of "elder" leadership it is not surprising that the infant churches were established with elders taking the lead. Our contemporary generation in the Western world no longer looks up to older people. Attention is directed in the opposite direction as is evidenced by the emphasis on trying to look young. It almost seems as if we should not admit that we're getting older because old age is to be shunned as undesirable. Society seems to suggest that older people are becoming increasingly redundant and should be placed in a safe, comfortable situation where they can quietly fade away with minimum fuss and bother. I believe this is a dangerous trend away from a fundamental biblical principle which teaches that as people get older they amass experience which produces a mature, balanced outlook on life. Without in any way detracting from the obvious youthful virtues of enthusiasm, idealism and energy, care should be taken to preserve the mature participation in leadership which experience alone provides.

Two important functions of the elders are emphasized by Peter. *The first is the shepherd function.* "Be shepherds of God's flock that is under your care" (1 Pet. 5:2). The Greek word for *shepherd* is also translated "pastor." When we talk about a pastor we're talking about a shepherd, and shepherding is an eldership responsibility.

Now Peter calls himself "a fellow elder," classifying himself with others who shared the responsibilities of leadership. No doubt, Peter's approach to shepherding was greatly influenced by the shepherding he received from the gracious Shepherd Himself. Having been carefully shepherded back into the fold after his dismal denial of Christ, Peter was himself appointed to be a shepherd.

Notice what he was required to do—"feed lambs," "feed sheep" and "shepherd sheep." One of the mistakes made in many churches is that we do not differentiate between "feeding lambs" and "feeding sheep." If the lamb loses its mother you pick it up, stick it under your arm, put a bottle in the lamb's mouth and you feed the lamb. But you don't put a large woolly sheep under your arm and encourage the smelly old thing to suck on bottles. But that's how many churches operate. Our church fully recognizes that there are people who are weak and wayward and far from the Shepherd. To them we present the Shepherd seeking to save them. When found by Him they become lambs who need some basic fundamental care. We need to spoon-feed them in the early days of spiritual growth. But as they grow into sheep they have to learn to feed themselves. The leadership, or shepherding, role in feeding must be clearly understood.

Shepherds of the sheep must also be leading as well as feeding. Note how our Lord said, "My sheep listen to my voice . . . and they follow me" (John 10:27). This is a strange concept to us because we have the idea of a flock of sheep being chased by a shepherd on a tractor shouting at a couple of sheep dogs. But in the Middle East they still shepherd the way they did 1,900 years ago. Little shepherd boys or girls playing on flutes wander over the barren wilderness and the sheep follow nose to tail! Wherever the shepherd goes they follow. One simple principle of the Christian church is that shepherds are leaders and leaders lead!

The independent spirit which pervades our society has infiltrated the church, producing sheep who won't be bothered with flocks, members of flocks who won't follow shepherds, and shepherds who have lost the nerve to lead! This is a gross caricature of the New Testament church, and both shepherds and sheep must bear part of the blame.

Secondly, Peter talks about the overseer function as well. The Greek words *presbuteros* (an elder) and *episcopos* (an overseer) are used interchangeably. Both terms are talking about the same kind of people involved in the same sort of functions. Leadership, therefore, not only "shepherds" but "oversees."

Overseeing involved "caring for" as is seen in Peter's words, "Be shepherds of God's flock that is under your care" (1 Pet. 5:2). God has ordained leadership in fellowships to care for sheep. Sheep are to gladly accept this care, not identifying it as interference.

In our society the wolves and the unscrupulous shepherds are after the sheep. Sheep, even though they've come to Christ, have not lost their sheep-ish tendencies! Therefore, in the flock of believers we must have people who are giving oversight, caring for souls.

Overseers also have a watching-out-for aspect to their ministry. Paul and Barnabas, after they had established churches, decided to "go back and visit the brothers . . . and see how they are doing" (Acts 15:36). The word translated "visit" is a derivative of *episcopos*. In other words, the leadership should be watching out for those under their care to see how they are doing! In churches large and small it is all too easy for people never to share, genuinely, how they're doing, either because they don't want anyone to know or because nobody cares enough to find out!

The Hebrew Epistle says, "See to it that no one misses the grace of God and that no bitter root grows up to cause trouble and defile many" (Heb. 12:15). This is relevant because the little expression "see to it" is also a derivative of *episcopos*. Overseers not only "watch out for" and "care for," but they also "see to it." They are the people who see to it that what needs to be done gets done in order that the church might be a church. It is clear from Scripture that we are called to build the church of Christ, under leadership that oversees and shepherds. This community of believers is to function in such a way that the risen Christ is patiently at work in the midst; and there is no escaping the fact that leadership is a major key to the success or failure of this God-given enterprise.

In light of this we need to consider not only the function of leadership but also the frailties of leadership. Elders are sheep just like the rest of the flock. All sheep have their problems but those in "leader-sheep" have their own problems and other people's too. While they handle their own frailties they must care for the frailties of others. Peter points out some obvious frailties.

First there are *frailties in attitude*. He said, "Be shepherds of God's flock . . . not because you must, but because you are willing" (1 Pet. 5:2). It's like pulling teeth to get some people to exercise leadership in the church of Jesus Christ; and sometimes those who do lead project an attitude of, "If I don't do it nobody else will." That kind of grudging leadership produces grumbling "followship." Leaders are called to lead with an attitude closer to enjoying it than enduring it.

Then there can be serious *frailties in motivation*. Why do we engage in leadership? Why do we shepherd? Why do we bother? Peter says, "Not greedy for money but eager to serve" (v. 2), so evidently he was encountering problems with some whose motivation was closer to "loot" than "love."

Frailties in "style" regularly surface in the church. Peter's emphasis is on "not lording it over those entrusted to you . . . being examples" (v. 3). Now there's a fine tension! Leaders have to lead, otherwise they are not leaders. But to some that means coming down on people with a steel hand and crushing them into submission. Others, more mature, accepting the fact of their own frailties, crave the support of other people to enable them to be examples of what should be done, rather than loud exhorters about what needs to be done!

Recently one of our elders, leading the congregation in prayer before I preached, said, "I hope Stuart has done his work this week. I hope he's been before God. I hope he's got a word from the Lord for us this morning. I hope he's prepared himself." It rejoiced my heart to be reminded that my leadership colleagues, knowing my frailties, don't criticize; they intercede for me before the throne that I might be a model, not a mogul.

Leadership is determined by followship. I'm not talking about whether leadership is good or bad. Some people are superb leaders but they're also wicked, so they lead people into wickedness. Others are very good people but rotten leaders because nobody follows them. Good or evil character does not determine leadership qualities, but whether or not anyone follows! When this is understood, the possible abuse of leadership positions becomes apparent. Church leaders need to ask themselves three questions: "Is anyone following me? and if so, where am I leading them? and if not, why do I see myself as a leader?"

No doubt leaders have always been confronted with problems. This was certainly the case for the church leaders to whom Peter wrote; but they, with leaders in all generations, should never lose sight of the "crown of glory" reserved for them by none other than "the Chief Shepherd."

TWENTY

THE MARKS OF MATURITY
1 Peter 5:5-14

Peter's Epistle, written against the dark background of impending crisis, leaves the unmistakable impression that if believers respond to the information and instructions contained therein they would behave in a mature fashion that would allow them to handle the tough situations well. The closing section of the Epistle contains a number of references to behavior patterns which we will call "marks of maturity"!

Maturity and Authority

There is, in the economy of God, an absolute necessity for order. For there to be order there must be authority which is recognized and respected. One of the marks of our maturity is the way we are prepared to accept authority and respond to it. Our secular society at the present time is suffering from a breakdown of authority. The unwillingness of people to accept authority is indicative of their immaturity, because thinking people recognize that a society without authority will sooner or later self-destruct. The same applies in the church, so we can identify spiritual maturity by the response, or lack of it, to authority in the fellowship of believers. Peter, therefore, tells the young men—which can mean young in age or young in the Lord—"Be submissive to those who are older" (1 Pet. 5:5). And this, as we have seen, does not necessarily mean older in years, but more mature in terms of leadership. Those who refuse to acknowledge authority show immaturity in their understanding of God's principles and lack of development in their spiritual and personal growth, which demand both discipline and a sense of responsibility.

Maturity and Humility

Peter goes on to say, "Clothe yourselves with humility toward one another, because, 'God opposes the proud but gives grace to the humble.' Humble yourselves, therefore, under God's mighty hand, that he may lift you up in due time" (vv. 5,6).

Humility is not spoken of as being something that some people have and some people don't have. It is the result of specific actions which are described by phrases such as, "Clothe yourselves with humility" and "Humble yourselves." What exactly do we mean by humility?

First of all, *humility is living with a realistic assessment of yourself.* Arrogant people have an unrealistic assessment of themselves. They think of themselves much more highly than they ought to think. But it is equally possible for us to think more "lowly" of ourselves than we ought to think! Therefore, genuinely humble people have a realistic assessment of themselves and live comfortably within that assessment. Christians ought to have a headstart in the realistic self-assessment department. Those who have a low self-image, who feel utterly worthless, must not confuse that position with humility or spiritual maturity. Every human being has tremendous worth because he was created by God in His image.

It is something of an insult to the Lord Jesus to feel that we have no value when He emphatically demonstrated that we were worth dying for. Redeemed, created beings have been made heirs of God and joint heirs with Christ. They have the post of ambassador in His diplomatic corps, fully aware that the Lord said, "In exactly the same way that the Father sent me so I am going to send you" (see John 20:21). It is not humility to pretend to be less than God has created, redeemed, commissioned and equipped us to be.

To maintain the balance, however, we need to remember that apart from God's creation we would not exist; without His redemption we would be lost; and apart from His call we would do nothing of eternal consequence. Genuinely humble people, knowing these things, avoid the ditch of unseemly arrogance on one side and the ditch of unwarranted self-denigration on the other, steering carefully up the middle of the road called *humility*. This we are called to do.

Secondly, *humility is the result of rejected pride*. Peter quotes Proverbs, "God opposes the proud but gives grace to the humble," with feeling, reinforced by his own painful proof of the statement's truth. Peter had a severe pride problem. Notice the ingredients of his pride. First of all, he sometimes talked as if he knew better than God.

When Jesus' truth conflicted with Peter's opinions, Peter won! The essence of pride is to contradict God! There is something in all of us which does that at one time or another, and we need to be very much aware of it, because genuine humility recognizes pride and deals with it thoroughly and conclusively. Peter's pride problem surfaced in the way he clearly felt superior to others. He was never slow to concede that his fellow disciples might fall away because of the obvious limitations from which they suffered and from which he was immune. Now that's pride!

Pride thinks grandly about self and Peter was good at that! Having been forewarned of his imminent denial of Christ, he spent his time denying any possibility of denial on his part. He seemed to feel that the Lord did not understand what he was made of. That was exactly the problem! Jesus did understand; it was Peter who didn't understand.

What is pride then? Pride is (1) to think grandly of our own capabilities apart from God, (2) to feel inordinately superior to others, and (3) to reject what God says and to decide to go our own way. No wonder God says, "Pride do I hate" (see 1 Pet. 5:5), because human history is littered with the wreckage of human pride.

God also resists the proud. The word used to describe God's action (*opposes*) is the word for a general getting all his armies lined up! In other words, God sees the proud person and commits Himself to marshaling His divine resources against that person to bring him down. That sounds very cruel of God, but it isn't, because knowing that proud people are out of touch with reality God commits Himself to bring them back to earth with a bump, if necessary, before their hot-air balloon bursts and they destroy themselves.

As a young boy I once heard the great American preacher Donald G. Barnhouse. I vividly remember his opening statement, "The way to up is down" and "the way to down is up." He was paraphrasing Peter in an unmistakably striking manner.

Thirdly, *humility is the result of resolute action*. The words translated "clothe yourselves with humility" mean, literally, "put on an apron." There is no question in my mind that Peter is thinking of the day Jesus took off His outer garment, picked up an apron or a towel, put it on, took a bowl of water to Peter and said, "You're first." And Peter said, "You're not going to wash my feet" only to be overruled and told that he didn't understand but would later (see John 13:2-10). At the time of this writing Peter understands, because the Lord Jesus had given him a very simple lesson in humility, which he had slowly learned. Humility is being prepared to serve. Pride is not being prepared to serve anybody, but expecting to be served. Humility is taking off the trappings and putting on the apron. Pride is totally immersing ourselves in ourselves, wrapping ourselves in ostentatious garments of self-indulgence. Peter's words bear repeating, "Humble yourselves, therefore, under God's mighty hand, that he may lift you up."

Maturity and Anxiety

There are degrees of anxiety. Normal anxiety is necessary. If somebody was not concerned enough to provide food and shelter many people would be cold and go hungry. Natural anxieties about safety, shelter and food are perfectly normal and totally necessary for survival. Then there is moderate anxiety that is motivating. Some people whose jobs are absolutely secure get paid whether they work or not. They know if they get fired they will be reinstated, so they don't produce. Others know if they don't produce they will be dismissed and there are plenty of people looking for jobs, so they work hard.

Now when the Bible says, "Cast all your anxiety on him because He cares for you" (1 Pet. 5:7) it is talking about excessive anxiety that is enervating. Peter had heard the Master speak about anxiety on the hills around Galilee. He remembered what He said about lilies being well dressed and birds being well fed because God cared for them. Peter had shown he was anxious about his position and recognition, about what would happen if he left his family. He got upset, worried and uptight all the time. Nervous tension built up in him, bursting out in anger and frustration. But somewhere he arrived at a solid conclusion that his God was God, that He cared and had promised to supply his needs and, therefore, while normal and moderate anxiety were necessary and healthy, extreme anxiety was out of order. That this was a conscious decision is shown by his use of the aorist tense meaning a radical once-and-for-all decision to trust and not be afraid, a decision which having been made would require constant reaffirmation.

Maturity and Sobriety

Peter's solemn words need to be treated with great seriousness, "Be self-controlled and alert. Your enemy the devil prowls around like a roaring lion looking for someone to devour. Resist him, standing firm in the faith, because you know that your brothers throughout the world are undergoing the same kind of sufferings" (vv. 8,9). A sober assessment of the situation in which believers live is of vital importance because the enemy of souls, the devil, is on a rampage. Now we tend to treat such statements rather lightly, but Peter is deadly earnest. He anticipates tremendous persecution and he sees behind this persecution an enemy of souls who is real and dangerous.

Not long ago the devil was laughed at, but relatively recently he has become very popular in contemporary books and movies. Sober evaluations of the fact that there is an enemy of our souls who is alive and sick on planet earth do not come from secular sources which portray him either as an implacable foe who reduces everyone to quivering terror, or a stand-up comedian shooting off one-liners. His name is *Diabolos*, which means "slanderer"—a name well earned from centuries of decimating the reputations of God's people, both in God's presence and among God's people.

A sober understanding of the forces of evil arrayed against us will include the insight that Christian reputation is destroyed by Christians doing the devil's work for him in the name of fellowship. Sobriety puts the phone down and announces, "This conversation stops forthwith." Always remember that having done all in his infernal power to stop you coming to Christ and failing, he can't get you back; but he will do all he can to stop you growing and maturing. Sober assessments of spiritual vulnerability and spiritual forces are marks of spiritual maturity.

Maturity and Stability
"And the God of all grace, who called you to his

eternal glory in Christ, after you have suffered a little while, will himself restore you and make you strong, firm and steadfast. To him be the power for ever and ever. Amen" (vv. 10,11). When the going gets tough for God's people He doesn't want us rocking and sinking without a trace. He wants us to exhibit that firmness, strength and steadfastness. How do we do it?

First, stability comes through *sensing the "mighty hand" of God (v. 6) upon our lives*. People submitted to Christ's enabling have a tremendous sense of stability because they know they stand firm in the mighty hand of God and in the eternal call of God. Notice that God calls us to His eternal glory after suffering a little while! The two aspects of the call of God—*to* eternal glory *through* earthly suffering—must not be separated.

We maintain stability when the going gets tough by *knowing that we'll finish up in glory having traveled a path of suffering*. There is no resurrection Christ without a cross—in the same way there is no eternal glory without some degree of earthly suffering. Deathbed conversions are better than no conversion, but do give the impression that, sensing the ship is sinking, those concerned bail out and get in God's lifeboat. This can be a gross misunderstanding of God's call. The call of God is not to live our own lives our own way and, at the last minute with our last breath, say whatever it takes to get Him to take us to eternal glory. The call of God involves earthly suffering because through it we magnify His power to keep us and demonstrate His grace in our weakness. Earthly suffering, bravely borne, shows powerfully the reality of the living God. When it is over we can lay down our weapons and enter into rest. This broad perspective provides the broad base upon which spiritual stability is built.

We also have stability through *standing in the grace of God.* I love the expression, "the God of all grace," even though it doesn't do justice to what Peter actually says. The word *all* means "many and varied types" of grace. Every kind of grace! God makes available every kind of grace for every kind of problem. There is nothing into which we will ever be called for which God does not have the right grace.

I am not a practical person when it comes to fixing things but I do enjoy periodic visits to hardware stores. Wandering along rows and rows of ingenious pieces of equipment I marvel at the variations of size, material, shape and purpose in which such common items as nails and screws are manufactured. There is a nail for every kind of hole, a screw for all conceivable fittings. God's store has every kind of grace for every kind of situation.

All these things are marks of maturity outlined by the apostle so that when the going gets tough those of us exposed to the toughness will have developed the Christian caliber necessary to withstand to the glory of God.

Other good reading from REGAL BOOKS: